WRITE
SOURCE

SkillsBook

EDITING AND PROOFREADING PRACTICE

. . . a resource of student activities
to accompany *Write Source*

WRITE SOURCE®

GREAT SOURCE EDUCATION GROUP
a Houghton Mifflin Company
Wilmington, Massachusetts

A Few Words About the *Write Source SkillsBook*

Before you begin . . .

The *SkillsBook* provides you with opportunities to practice editing and proofreading skills. *Write Source* contains guidelines, examples, and models to help you complete your work in the *SkillsBook*.

Each *SkillsBook* activity includes a brief introduction to the topic and examples showing how to complete that activity. You will be directed to the page numbers in *Write Source* for additional information and examples. The "Proofreading Activities" focus on punctuation, the mechanics of writing, usage, and spelling. The "Sentence Activities" provide practice in sentence combining and in correcting common sentence problems. The "Language Activities" highlight each of the eight parts of speech.

Most exercises include a **Next Step** activity at the end of the exercise. The purpose of the Next Step activity is to provide ideas that will help you apply what you have learned in your own writing.

Authors: Pat Sebranek and Dave Kemper

Printed in the United States of America

International Standard Book Number: 978-0-669-51818-4 (student edition)

4 5 6 7 8 9 10 -POO- 10 09 08 07

International Standard Book Number: 978-0-669-51823-8 (teacher's edition)

2 3 4 5 6 7 8 9 10 -POO- 10 09 08 07 06

Table of Contents

Proofreading Activities

Using Punctuation

Checking Mechanics

Proofreading Activities

Checking Your Spelling

Using the Right Word

Sentence Activities

Sentence Basics

Sentence Problems

Sentence Combining

Language Activities

Nouns

Pronouns

Verbs

Adjectives and Adverbs

Prepositions, Conjunctions, Interjections

Parts of Speech

1

Proofreading Activities

The activities in this section include sentences that need to be checked for punctuation, mechanics, and usage. Each activity includes a link to a page or pages in *Write Source* to be used as a guide for the activity.

Name _____

Periods 1

Write Source Link

447

A **period** is just a little dot, but it has a lot of important uses.

● For one thing, a period is used at the end of a sentence that makes a **statement**.

Frogs begin their lives in the water.
Later, they live on land.
Frogs are amphibians.

● A period is also used at the end of a **request**.

Please look up "amphibian" in the dictionary.
Find out what the word means.

1

Put an *S* in front of each statement, and put an *R* in front of each request. End each sentence with a period. The first one has been done for you.

___S___ **1.** Most frogs are expert swimmers.

_____ **2.** Frogs get much of their power from their strong back legs

_____ **3.** Do the frog kick next time you are in the water

_____ **4.** Draw your legs up to your sides

_____ **5.** Then push them straight back

_____ **6.** You will move forward just as a frog does

_____ **7.** You might enjoy swimming this way

_____ **8.** Frogs wouldn't swim in any other way

2 The following paragraph has nine sentences in it. Find the nine sentences. Put a capital letter at the beginning of each one and a period at the end of each one. The first sentence has been done for you.

S̶ome frogs have homes that are high off the ground⊙

these frogs live in trees tree frogs like leafy homes many tree

frogs are green not all of them are green some are yellow, red,

or orange others have stripes and spots tree frogs live in all

parts of the world you may have some in your neighborhood

Next Step Write two sentences. In the first one, state something that a frog can do. In the second one, tell a friend to do something that a frog does.

1. *Statement* _____

_____

_____

2. *Request* _____

_____

_____

Name _____

Periods 2

Put a **period** after an initial in a person's name. Also use a period after an abbreviation and to separate dollars and cents.

Carl B. Picklefoot   M. Jennifer Jump

Mr. Picklefoot   Foster Ave.

$1.25 $11.00

Write Source Link

447

1 Put periods after the initials in Samantha's name. Then write your name in all of these ways.

Samantha R   _____

Samantha J Rowe   _____

S J Rowe   _____

S J R   _____

2 Put periods after the abbreviations in these sentences.

1. Where does Mr Brown live?

2. He used to live on W Water St , but now he has moved.

3. His new home is on E Carver Ave , next door to Ms Trout.

4. Ms Trout is a dentist, so she is also Dr Trout.

5. One of Mr Brown's other neighbors is Lt O'Malley, a police officer.

6. Many of the homes on E Carver Ave were built by J J Builders.

3 Add 11 periods where they belong in the paragraph below. The first sentence has been done for you.

Mr. Henry J. Picklefoot went to E. Lancaster to visit his cousin, Ms. Mary W. Bristle. Ms Bristle works at a movie theater in E Lancaster. The theater is on W Broad St , just past J J Pollacco's Pizza Palace. While Ms Bristle was working, Mr Picklefoot went to three movies. Each one cost $7 00. The next day, Mr Picklefoot decided to go back home to W Lancaster. He had seen enough movies.

4 Write the following amounts as numbers with dollar signs and periods to separate dollars and cents.

1. Ten dollars and twenty-nine cents _____

2. One hundred dollars and two cents _____

3. Two dollars and seventy-three cents _____

4. Forty dollars and no cents _____

5. Ninety-nine dollars and ninety-nine cents _____

6. Eighteen dollars and thirty-six cents _____

Next Step Write two names that include abbreviations or initials. Write two numbers with dollars and cents. (You can find this information in a magazine or newspaper.) Then write two sentences using these names and numbers.

Name _____

End Punctuation

Write Source Link

447, 448

- A **question mark** follows a question.
  Do you want broccoli for supper?

- An **exclamation point** follows a word or
  sentence that shows strong feeling.
  Wow! That's a great idea!

- A **period** follows a statement or a request.
  I'm not sure I heard you. Say that again.

1 Put a period, a question mark, or an exclamation point at the end of each of these sentences.

1. What's good about broccoli _____

2. Broccoli is rich in vitamins _____

3. It tastes great _____

4. It has a pretty green color _____

5. The home gardener finds it easy to grow _____

6. Why doesn't everyone eat broccoli _____

7. I like it with cheese sauce _____

8. Who likes it raw _____

9. I do _____ I do _____

10. Broccoli is definitely my favorite vegetable _____

8

2 **Put a question mark, an exclamation point, or a period at the end of each sentence in this paragraph.**

My favorite vegetable is carrots They're so sweet Do you know how my little brother eats carrots He puts them in rolls and eats them like hot dogs It's gross What is your favorite vegetable Do you like carrots, too

Next Step **Write three sentences about one of the vegetables listed below. One sentence should make a statement or request, another sentence should ask a question, and the third one should express strong feeling.**

eggplant   cabbage   asparagus   squash   corn

1. *Statement* _____

_____

_____

2. *Question* _____

_____

_____

3. *Exclamation* _____

_____

_____

Name _____

Commas Between Items in a Series

Write Source Link

450

● Use commas between words in a series.
Most desks are full of <u>papers</u>, <u>pencils</u>, and <u>books</u>.

● Use commas between phrases in a series.
My dad uses solar <u>calculators</u>, <u>felt-tip pens</u>, and <u>sticky notes</u>.

 In each sentence, put commas between the words and phrases in the series.

1. My mom's desk is covered with letters bills and pictures.

2. Paper clips safety pins and thumbtacks are in a jar.

3. She keeps rulers scissors and a plant on a shelf.

4. The top drawer holds stickers rubber bands two checkbooks and three notepads.

5. The bottom drawer contains spiral notebooks file folders and old letters.

6. She keeps pencils pens and markers in a can that I made in school.

7. A dictionary a world atlas and two telephone directories are placed on another shelf.

Next Step Make a list of things you have in your desk or locker.

_____   _____

_____   _____

_____   _____

_____   _____

_____   _____

Now write a paragraph about the things in your desk or locker. Begin with this topic sentence: Please don't open this desk! Your sentences should include words or phrases in a series.

_____

_____

_____

_____

_____

_____

_____

_____

_____

Name _____

Commas in Letter Writing

Use a comma after a greeting in a letter and after the closing.

Write Source Link

- A postcard

July 12

Dear Sally,
I went to the zoo today. I saw a funny-looking anteater.
I wish you could see it, too!

Your friend,

Suzie

SALLY KASTEN
143 WHITE ST
LINCOLN NE 68500

 1 Write your own postcard message below. Be sure to add a date and sign your name. Use commas correctly.

Name
_____

Commas to Keep Numbers Clear

Write Source Link
450

Commas are used in numbers to make them easier to read. If there are four or more numbers, use a comma.

There are about 1,500 trees in the city park.

That old car only cost $2,500 when it was new.

Hint: Don't use commas in numbers that represent a year (1776, 2010).

 In the following sentences, add commas to keep the numbers clear. If the number does not need a comma, circle the number. The first one has been done for you.

1. Our teacher told me that our school has 1728 students.

2. Some United States Navy ships have a crew of 5000 people.

3. The principal said that 300 parents came to our talent show.

4. Someone gave $2500 to the school for new drums.

5. My mother paid $25 for my new backpack.

6. The wall near the school playground has 3200 bricks in it.

Next Step **Add commas to the numbers below where needed.**

1. the year 2000   **3.** 3250 people   **5.** $4555

2. 290 boxes   **4.** 1475 tickets   **6.** 2312 computers

Name _____

Commas in Dates and Addresses

Write Source Link

HAPPY BIRTHDAY

452

1 Write the names, addresses, and birth dates (including the year) for three of your classmates or friends. Be sure to use commas correctly.

Name _____

Address _____

City, State, ZIP _____

Birth Date _____

Name _____

Address _____

City, State, ZIP _____

Birth Date _____

Name _____

Address _____

City, State, ZIP _____

Birth Date _____

2 Complete each invitation below. Use the names and addresses from the first page in this activity. (Feel free to decorate the invitations.)

SURPRISE PARTY

Please come to a surprise party for

_____

Date: _____

Time: _____

Address: _____

_____

Neighborhood Picnic

Please join _____

for an afternoon of fun.

Address: _____

_____

Date: _____

Time: _____

Name _____

Commas in
Compound Sentences

452

Use a **comma** before the connecting word in a compound sentence. Some common connecting words are *and, but,* and *or.*

> I study plants in school, and I know a lot about them.

> I've read about the Venus flytrap, but I've never seen one.

1   **Underline the connecting word in each of these compound sentences. Put a comma before each connecting word.**

1. Most plants get their food from soil but some plants eat insects.

2. The Venus flytrap grows in swamps and it really is a trap for flies.

3. The flytrap looks harmless but it is a danger zone for bugs.

4. The leaves are like traps and they actually have teeth!

5. An insect lands on a flytrap's leaf and the leaf snaps shut.

6. The insect is trapped and it can't get away.

7. Venus flytraps are grown in plant stores or they grow wild.

8. You can feed your Venus flytrap bugs but you shouldn't feed it meat.

9. Meat has salt in it and Venus flytraps don't like salt.

2 Combine each pair of simple sentences to make a compound sentence. Put a comma before the connecting word. The first one has been done for you.

1. Computers are fast.
   They are fun to use.

   Computers are fast, and they are fun to use.

2. Robin wants to use her new computer.
   She does not know how to turn it on.

3. She needs help fast.
   She will cry.

4. Robin asks Ms. Kadiddle.
   She says she will help.

Next Step Write a compound sentence about using a computer.

Name _____

Write Source Link

Commas to Set Off a Speaker's Words

Use a **comma** to set off the exact words of a speaker from the rest of the sentence.

454

Ms. Ayala asked, "Who remembers the story of the wolf and the kid?"

"I think I do," answered Jamal.

1 Put commas where they are needed in these sentences.

1. "It was about a mother goat who went to get food for her kid" Jamal said.

2. "That's the beginning" said Sam. "Then the mother told the kid to lock the door and not let anyone in."

3. "Next a wolf knocks on the door and talks sweet like the mother" Jamal said.

4. Sam continued "The kid peeks through the window and sees the wolf."

5. "And he doesn't let the wolf in" said Jamal.

6. Ms. Ayala said "What lesson can you learn from this story?"

7. "Mothers know best" laughed Sam and Jamal.

Next Step Write one more thing Ms. Ayala could have said about the story. Be sure to use a comma where it is needed.

_____

_____

2 Put commas where they are needed in the following sentences.

1. "Let's think of other fables we've read" said the teacher.

2. Jan replied "I remember the one about the ant and

the grasshopper."

3. "Oh, that's where the ant does all the work and the

grasshopper is lazy" said Amy.

4. "Yes" said Jan. "The ant saved food for the winter, while the

grasshopper wasted time."

5. "There's a lesson there" said the teacher.

6. Amy said "I think it means we should do our work on time."

7. "Good thinking" said the teacher.

Next Step Write one more thing the teacher might say. Use a comma and quotation marks in your sentence.

_____

Name

Commas After an Introductory Word

Write Source Link

454

- Use a **comma** to set off the name of a person or group being spoken to.
  Class, we're starting an all-drum band.

- Use a comma to set off an interjection.
  Gosh, that will make a loud noise!

1   Add commas where they are needed in these sentences.

1. Josh you play the conga drum.

2. Yolanda you take the tom-tom.

3. Tony here's a tabla drum for you.

4. Wow you sure can play the big bass drum, Elle.

5. Help I can't lift this big drum.

6. Look that drum is taller than I am.

7. George can you play a bongo drum?

8. Carla you play the triangle.

9. Our teacher said, "Wait I want everyone to stay after practice."

Next Step Imagine that your class is going to have a band with many different instruments. Write four sentences, each telling a person to play an instrument. (Choose from the instruments below, or come up with your own.) Make sure to use commas correctly. One has been done for you.

maracas	guitar	flute
tambourine	banjo	piano

1. Todd, you play the tambourine. _____

2. _____

   _____

   _____

3. _____

   _____

   _____

4. _____

   _____

   _____

5. _____

   _____

   _____

Name _____

Commas After a Group of Words

Write Source Link
454

● Use a **comma** to set off an introductory group of words.

After school, I play with my friends.

When it gets too dark, we all head for home.

1 Add commas where they are needed in the following sentences. Three sentences do not need commas.

1. Because it was dark the playground was closed.

2. I rode my bike around the block.

3. When my mom came home I gave her a big hug.

4. After supper we played catch.

5. I like to drink hot cocoa before bedtime.

6. While I brushed my teeth my dad talked about our fishing trip.

7. Before I went to sleep I read my favorite book.

8. During the night I dreamed about catching huge fish.

9. In the morning my mom asked me if I wanted sardines for breakfast.

10. I think I was still dreaming.

2 Complete the sentences below. Make sure you add a comma after the introductory words. The first one has been done for you.

1. When lightning flashes in the sky, _I listen for the loud boom of_ the thunder.

2. After the rain starts falling _____

_____

_____

3. During the storm _____

_____

_____

4. Because my dog doesn't like thunder _____

_____

_____

5. Until the sun shines again _____

_____

_____

Name _____

Apostrophes 1

An **apostrophe** is used in the spelling of a contraction. The apostrophe takes the place of one or more letters.

Two Words	Contraction
did not	didn't
you are	you're
I am	I'm

apostrophes

456

1 Write a contraction for each word or word pair in the list. Then rewrite each sentence, replacing the words in bold letters with a contraction.

Two Words	Contraction
is not	_____
it is	_____
do not	_____
they are	_____
cannot	_____

1. Mary **cannot** sing. Mary can't sing. _____

2. Jake **is not** singing. _____

3. **They are** both not singing. _____

4. **It is** time for you to sing. _____

5. But I **do not** want to. _____

2 Write contractions for the following word pairs.

Two Words	Contraction	Two Words	Contraction
1. it is; it has	_____	8. will not	_____
2. they will	_____	9. I would	_____
3. do not	_____	10. who is	_____
4. I am	_____	11. there is	_____
5. I have	_____	12. could not	_____
6. is not	_____	13. was not	_____
7. you are	_____	14. did not	_____

3 In each sentence below, write a contraction to replace the words in bold.

1. **They will** be riding six white horses when she comes. _____

2. **It is** just like a magic penny. _____

3. But the cat came back: it just **could not** stay away. _____

4. If **you are** happy and you know it, clap your hands. _____

5. **There is** a hole in the bottom of the sea. _____

6. **I have** been working on the railroad. _____

7. **Who is** afraid of the big, bad wolf? _____

8. **I am** a little teapot short and stout. _____

Next Step The sentences above are lines from songs. Can you sing any of them?

Name _____

Write Source Link

Apostrophes 2

An **apostrophe** plus an **s** is added to a singular noun to show ownership. (Singular means "one.")

the girl's bike (The bike belongs to the girl.)
the cat's whiskers
(The whiskers belong to the cat.)

458

1 In each sentence, put an apostrophe in the word that tells who the gerbil belongs to. The first one has been done for you.

1. Chesters gerbil likes leaf lettuce.

2. I think LaJoys gerbil is the cutest.

3. Where is the teachers gerbil?

4. Mollys gerbil is under my desk!

5. My neighbors gerbil stays in a cage.

2 In each sentence, draw a line under the word that tells who the hat belongs to. Draw one of the hats in the box.

1. Who has the baby's hat?

2. Mr. Dandelion's hat is yellow.

3. Look at Roger's hat!

4. Did you see Kathy's red hat?

5. Rocky Stark's hat is black.

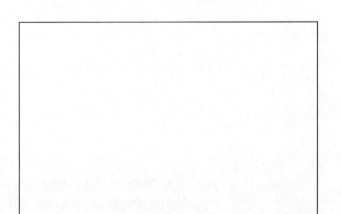

3 Combine each set of words into a possessive phrase. Then write an interesting sentence using the phrase. Make sure to use apostrophes correctly. The first one has been done for you.

1. Betty ➤ house ___Betty's house___

___I went to Betty's house to play.___

2. my sister ➤ pony _____

_____

3. our dog ➤ name _____

_____

4. a clown ➤ face _____

_____

5. Mr. Brown ➤ car _____

_____

6. a bluebird ➤ house _____

_____

7. Shauna ➤ desk _____

_____

Next Step Exchange your sentences with a classmate. Check the apostrophes in your partner's work.

Name _____

Write Source Link

458

ROVER

Apostrophes 3

● Add **'s** to a singular noun to show ownership. (Singular means "one.")

the dog's house

● Add an apostrophe after a plural noun ending in **s**. (Plural means "more than one.")

the dogs' houses

1 Add an apostrophe in each phrase below to show ownership. In the blank, tell if the phrase shows singular or plural possession. The first one has been done for you.

1. Maryanne has one hamster in a cage. You write . . .

the hamster's cage _____ singular possession _____

2. Claudia has a cage with three hamsters in it. You write . . .

the hamsters cage _____

3. You have a rabbit. The rabbit lives in a hutch. You write . . .

the rabbits hutch _____

4. Your brother gets a rabbit, so you have two rabbits. You write . . .

the rabbits hutch _____

5. The rabbits have babies. You have to get another hutch. You write . . .

the rabbits hutches _____

2 Put a possessive singular noun in the blank to complete each sentence. The first sentence has been done for you.

1. _____Madeline's_____ dog ate my lunch.

2. My _____ dog likes potato chips.

3. _____ dog barked at me.

4. Where is _____ little dog?

5. I have to walk _____ dog for a week.

Next Step Below is a list of names and the things that belong to each person or group. Combine the two words into a possessive phrase. Then write an interesting sentence using the phrase. The first one has been done for you.

1. Katie ➤ roller skates _Katie's roller skates_

Katie's roller skates have lightning bolts painted on them.

2. Mr. Frank ➤ cane _____

_____

3. Dolly ➤ wig _____

_____

4. the Dolphins ➤ helmets _____

_____

5. Diana ➤ gowns _____

_____

Name _____

Write Source Link

Quotation Marks 1

One way to show what people say to each other is to use speech balloons.

Why didn't you call me back last night?

I'm sorry. We got home very late.

Another way to show what people say is to use **quotation marks**. The quotation marks set off the exact words of the speaker.

Tom said, "Why didn't you call me back last night?"
"I'm sorry. We got home very late," Les answered.

1 **Read the words in the speech balloons below. Then, in the sentences that follow, put quotation marks before and after the exact words that Tom and Les said.**

I wanted to ask if you could sleep over Saturday night.

I hope I can. I'll ask my mom.

Tom said, I wanted to ask if you could sleep over

Saturday night.

I hope I can. I'll ask my mom, said Les.

2 Read the speech balloons that follow. Then, in the space below, write what Tom and Les said, using quotation marks correctly in your sentences.

> My dad and I are going to set up the tent in our yard.

> Great! I'll bring my sleeping bag.

Tom said, _____

_____

_____

Les replied, _____

_____

_____

Next Step It's the next day. Tom and Les see each other again. Now you decide what they say. Make sure to use quotation marks correctly.

_____

_____

_____

_____

Name _____

Write Source Link

460

Quotation Marks 2

When you write **dialogue**, you can name the speaker at the beginning of the sentence, at the end of the sentence, or in the middle of the sentence.

● When the speaker is named at the **beginning** of the sentence, use a comma and quotation marks like this:

Carla said, "I'm going to camp this summer."

● When the speaker is named at the **end** of the sentence, use a comma and quotation marks like this:

"Late at night, we tell ghost stories," said Camy.

● When the speaker is named in the **middle** of the sentence, use commas and quotation marks like this:

"Camp starts July 5," Carla said, "and we stay for two weeks."

1 Add commas and quotation marks where they are needed in the following sentences. The speaker is named at the beginning of each sentence.

1. Camy said I'm going, too.

2. Josh said Won't you miss your parents?

3. Carla answered Yes, but we'll still have fun.

4. Josh asked What are you going to take?

5. Carla said I'm taking a lot of shorts and T-shirts.

2 Add commas and quotation marks in the sentences below. The speaker is named at the end of each sentence.

1. The ghost stories always scare me a little Camy said.

2. I'd be scared, too said Josh.

3. Aw, they're only fake stories said Carla.

3 Add commas and quotation marks in the following sentences. The speaker is named in the middle of each sentence.

1. This summer said Carla I'm going to learn to dive.

2. I can dive Camy said but not headfirst.

3. If it's not headfirst said Josh it's not a dive.

4. If it's belly first Josh said it's a belly flop!

Next Step Write two more sentences of dialogue between the campers. Use commas and quotation marks correctly to punctuate your dialogue.

_____

_____

_____

_____

_____

Name _____

Quotation Marks, Underlining, and Italics to Punctuate Titles

Write Source Link

460, 462

When you write, put quotation marks around titles of songs, short stories, and poems. Underline the titles of books, movies, TV programs, plays, and magazines and the names of ships and aircraft. (Use italics instead of underlining if you write with a computer).

We sang "The Star-Spangled Banner" before the game.

Marie read the poem "Clouds on a Windy Day."

Al liked the story "Babbling Brook."

I watched the movie *Bambi* with my little sister. (Bambi)

I enjoyed reading the magazine *Cricket*. (Cricket)

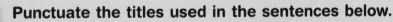

1   **Punctuate the titles used in the sentences below.**

1. Ali likes to read the magazine National Geographic.

2. My friends watched the movie Peter Pan.

3. Our class read the short story The Mountain.

4. We sang the song Row, Row, Row Your Boat five times.

5. My mother bought the book Airborn.

6. Jamie likes the TV show called Bill Nye the Science Guy.

7. Ona, Cloud Rider is a great short story.

8. The Nina, Pinta, and Santa Maria were Columbus' ships.

2 **In each sentence below, punctuate the title with quotation marks or underlining.**

1. Yoko went to see the movie The Incredibles.

2. The Ranger Rick magazine is filled with facts about animals.

3. Sylvia's dad bought her a book called The Tale of Despereaux.

4. Everybody sang Old MacDonald Had a Farm.

5. Joann says she likes the Muppets on Sesame Street.

6. Sammy smiles when he reads the poem Three Words.

7. Phil's family bought Spider-Man 2 in the DVD version.

8. Flat Stanley is one of Josie's favorite books.

9. Do you like this magazine? It's called Highlights.

Next Step **Write two sentences. Each should include the title of a song, a book, a movie, or a magazine. Be sure to punctuate the titles correctly.**

_____

_____

_____

_____

_____

Name _____

Colons

- Use a **colon** after the salutation of a business letter.

  Dear Ms. Cosby: Dear Sir:

- Use a colon between the hours and the minutes in a number that shows time.

  1:15   12:30

---

1 **Add colons as they are needed in the business letter below.**

Dear Mayor Hudson

I am writing to let you know about our neighborhood's "Cleanup Day." It will

take place on Saturday, April 17, from 1 0 0 0 a.m. to 4 0 0 p.m. City trucks

will be needed at the following times and places:

1 1 3 0 a.m.   City trucks needed to begin picking up bagged trash. It will

be placed at street corners throughout the neighborhood.

1 2 0 0 noon   Lunch will be donated by El Taco Grande.

4 0 0 p.m.   City trucks needed to pick up brush cleared at Green Bayou

Park. Brush will be piled at the park entrance.

Thank you for your help with this project.

Sincerely,

Matt Stone

Matt Stone

2 Below are the beginnings of some business letters. Students wrote these letters to confirm plans for field trips. Add colons where they are needed in the letters.

1. Dear Fire Chief Wilson

Our class is looking forward to visiting the fire station next Monday from 9 3 0 until 1 1 0 0 a.m.

2. Dear Ms. Stephanopoulos

Thank you for inviting us to visit your bakery on Friday between 1 0 3 0 a.m. and 1 2 0 0 noon.

3. Dear Ms. Kennedy

Our class is excited about visiting the TV station from 1 0 0 until 2 0 0 p.m. next Friday.

4. Dear Mr. Alvarez

We are looking forward to our tour of the stadium next Thursday between 1 1 0 0 a.m. and 1 2 3 0 p.m.

Next Step Write the beginning of a letter about a field trip. Write your letter to someone who works at a place you would like to visit. (Make up his or her name.)

_____

_____

_____

Name _____

Hyphens

You can use a hyphen to divide a word into syllables. Do this when you run out of room at the end of a line.

dra-gon-fly

I ran outside when I saw the dragon-fly on the porch.

Write Source Link

466

1 Divide the words below by using a hyphen between the syllables.

1. kitten _____

2. picture _____

3. wagon _____

4. people _____

5. music _____

6. helpless _____

7. kitchen _____

8. hyphen _____

9. movie _____

10. window _____

Name _____

Write Source Link
466

Parentheses

You can use parentheses to add information to your writing.

Use two nails (two inches long) for each side of the box.

Yesterday, I spotted an unusual bird (a brown creeper).

 1 In the sentences below, add parentheses where they are needed.

1. Mike read about birds in the encyclopedia volume 2.

2. Lee the second boy on the right has three dogs.

3. Store the footballs in the locker green box behind the door.

4. You can read the poem in this book see chapter 3.

5. Reg's house is on Water Street check my map.

6. To paint the model, follow the directions see the back of the box.

Next Step Write a sentence about the weather that includes parentheses to add information.

_____

_____

_____

Name _____

Punctuation Review

Write Source Link
447-466

This activity is a review of punctuation marks.

 1 Fill in the blanks in the following sentences. Make sure to use punctuation marks correctly.

1. Today's date is _____ .

2. My school's name is _____ .

My school is in this city and state:

_____

3. School starts at _____ a.m., and it ends at _____ p.m.

4. Our class is studying _____

_____ and _____ .

5. Our teacher's name is _____ .

2 Fill in the blanks in the following sentences. Show each speaker's exact words. Make sure to use commas and quotation marks correctly.

1. My teacher asked me _____

_____

2. I answered _____

_____

3 In the letter below, add the needed punctuation (commas, periods, parentheses, hyphens, and so on).

April 23 2005

Dear Ramos

After I called you last week I watched the movie Robots The trip through the robot city was amazing. Did you see that movie Josie said that more than 500 kids in our town have seen it. Thats a lot of kids When you come to visit me in July maybe we can rent the movie. I would like to see it again.

Im working on a model ship see the drawing on the back of this letter. It is a nuclear submarine. Its the newest sub marine called the Seawolf. My stepfather is helping me put it together. I will paint it black rust and silver.

I have to go do my homework now. I hope you have fun playing soccer. Lets practice kicking goals when youre here.

Your friend

Brian

Name _____

Capitalizing Proper Nouns

A **proper noun** names a specific person, place, thing, or idea. A proper noun is always capitalized.

Mary

St. Louis

Strawberry Festival

470, 472, 516

1 Write two proper nouns for each category.

1. city _____Houston_____   _____Springfield_____

2. holiday _____   _____

3. school _____   _____

4. ocean _____   _____

5. person _____   _____

6. park _____   _____

2 Write an interesting sentence using at least two of the proper nouns in your list.

_____

_____

_____

_____

3 Fill in the missing days and months in the two charts below. Remember that days and months are capitalized.

Days of the Week

1. _____Monday_____
2. _____
3. _____Wednesday_____

4. _____
5. _____
6. _____Saturday_____
7. _____

Months of the Year

1. _____
2. _____February_____
3. _____
4. _____April_____
5. _____
6. _____

7. _____
8. _____August_____
9. _____
10. _____October_____
11. _____
12. _____December_____

Next Step Answer the following questions.

1. What day and month is it today?

_____

2. In what month were you born? _____

3. What is your favorite day of the week? _____

Name _____

Capitalizing First Words

Write Source **Link**

472

● Always capitalize the **first word** in a sentence.

My heart is a muscle.

Can you hear it beat?

● Capitalize the first word of a direct quotation, too.
(A quotation is the words spoken by someone.)

She said, "Only I can hear it."

1 **Capitalize the first word in each sentence below. The first one has been done for you.**

1. E̶very animal has a pulse rate.

2. it is measured in heartbeats per minute.

3. big animals have slower pulse rates than little animals.

4. find your pulse.

5. how fast is your heart beating?

6. what do you mean?

7. count the number of times your heart beats in one minute.

8. the average person's heart beats 72 times a minute.

9. runners may have heart rates as low as 35 beats per minute.

10. that's so low!

2 Add capital letters where they are needed in the sentences below. The first one has been done for you.

1. "Ḣow fast does your heart beat?" he asked.

2. she answered, "my heartbeat is not as fast as a baby's."

3. he said, "how fast is a baby's heartbeat?"

4. "it's not as fast as a rabbit's," she said.

5. then he asked, "how fast is a rabbit's heartbeat?"

6. She smiled and said, "it's not as fast as a mouse's."

Next Step Write a paragraph explaining why the heart is a sign of love. Make sure to capitalize and punctuate your sentences correctly.

_____

_____

_____

_____

_____

_____

_____

Name _____

Capitalizing Titles

Capitalize the first word of the **title** of a book or magazine, the last word, and every important word in between.

<u>The Biggest Pancake Ever</u> **(book title)**

Follow these rules for words in the middle of a title.
- Don't capitalize articles *(a, an, the)*.
- Don't capitalize short prepositions *(to, with, by, for)*.
- Don't capitalize conjunctions *(and, but)*.

<u>Tea with Milk</u> (book)

<u>Amelia and Eleanor Go for a Ride</u> (book)

1 Write the titles using capital letters in the right places. Because these are names of books and magazines, underline them. The first one has been done for you.

1. the cat and the fiddle   <u>The Cat and the Fiddle</u>

2. penny pollard's letters _____

3. i'm in charge of celebrations

_____

4. the dragon's boy _____

5. song of the trees _____

6. ranger rick _____

7. highlights for children _____

2 Follow each direction by adding titles. Use capital letters correctly. Underline the titles.

 Two of my favorite TV shows:

_____

_____

 Two of my favorite books:

_____

_____

_____

 Two of my favorite movies:

_____

_____

_____

✔ **When I write my first book, the title will be one of these three:**

_____

_____

_____

Name

Capitalizing Geographic Names

The names of specific rivers, lakes, mountains, cities, states, countries, streets, roads, planets, and highways should be capitalized.

1 Write three geographic names in each of the columns. Be sure to use capital letters correctly. (You may want to work on this activity with a partner.)

Rivers	Lakes

Cities	States

Streets/Avenues	Planets

48

Capitalize the geographic names in these sentences. The numbers in parentheses tell you how many capital letters you need to change. The first sentence has been done for you.

1. The town of R̸ed L̸ion, P̸ennsylvania, is on the S̸usquehanna
   R̸iver. *(5)*

2. If you're looking for lake old wives, you'll find it in canada. *(4)*

3. The hungry horse reservation is in montana. *(4)*

4. The snake river forms part of the border between idaho
   and oregon. *(4)*

5. There's a town in arkansas called bad knob. *(3)*

6. In ohio you'll find mount healthy. *(3)*

7. If you ever go to flaydada, texas, you might see the salt
   fork river. *(5)*

8. When pumpkin creek joins the tongue river, they flow into
   the yellowstone river. *(6)*

9. In new jersey you'll find a city called orange. *(3)*

10. You'll find lake cadibarrawirracanna in australia. *(3)*

11. The honey river flows through california. *(3)*

Name _____

Capitalization Review

This activity is a review of capitalization.

Write Source Link

470, 472, 474

1 Add capital letters in the following paragraphs. Also answer the question after each paragraph. The first capital letter has been added.

Rub It Out

In 1770, an englishman named joseph priestley was traveling in south america.   he gathered some of the juice coming from the trees.   he found that it would rub out pencil marks.   he called it rubber.

What are three things that are made of rubber?

_____   _____   _____

Blast It

in sweden, a man named alfred nobel invented a blasting material he called dynamite.   miners often use dynamite.   money he earned from the invention now goes to people who win the nobel prize.

Why do miners use dynamite?

_____

_____

Here are two more paragraphs to capitalize. Also answer the question at the end of each paragraph.

Weave It

long ago, empress si ling-chi was sipping tea in china. a caterpillar cocoon fell into her cup. she unwound the cocoon and said, "it's made of a long thread. what will happen if I have it woven into cloth?" that's how chinese silk was discovered.

What are two things that are made of silk?

_____   _____

Wipe It Off

an american woman, mary anderson, had a good idea in 1903. "aha!" she thought. "if you push a rubber blade across a windshield, you can wipe away rain and snow." what do we call her invention today?

Answer: _____

Name _____

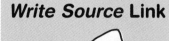 **Write Source** Link

Plurals 1

A **plural noun** names more than one thing. Most plurals are formed by adding *s* to the word. But some nouns form their plurals in different ways.

- The plurals of nouns ending in **sh, ch, x, s,** or **z** are made by adding *es* to the singular.
  brush → brushes   fox → foxes   glass → glasses

- The plurals of nouns that end in **y** with a consonant just before the **y** are formed by changing the **y** to **i** and adding **es.**
  baby → babies   fly → flies

- The plurals of nouns that end in **y** with a vowel just before the **y** are formed by adding only an **s.**
  day → days   monkey → monkeys

1 Write the plural form for each singular noun. The first two have been done for you.

1. boss   _bosses_   **7.** army   _____

2. rabbit   _rabbits_   **8.** plane   _____

3. mess   _____   **9.** sky   _____

4. dish   _____   **10.** donkey   _____

5. fox   _____   **11.** switch   _____

6. ant   _____   **12.** buzz   _____

2 Write the correct plurals in the blanks. The first sentence has been done for you.

1. Long ago twin __princesses__ lived in a palace.
  (princess)

2. One night two old _____ came to the gate.
  (lady)

3. Each lady carried a pile of _____ .
  (box)

4. "Each box holds three _____ ," they said.
  (wish)

5. The young _____ opened the gate.
  (princess)

Next Step Write a short ending to the story started above.

_____

_____

_____

_____

_____

_____

_____

Name _____

Plurals 2

A **plural noun** names more than one thing. In this activity, you will practice forming many different plural nouns. (You may use a dictionary with this activity.)

476

1 Write the plural form for each word listed below.

1. bunch _____

2. box _____

3. pitch _____

4. day _____

5. story _____

6. daddy _____

7. beach _____

8. glass _____

9. guess _____

10. flash _____

11. jelly _____

12. key _____

13. candy _____

14. baby _____

2 Write the plural form for each irregular noun below.

1. wolf _____

2. knife _____

3. mouse _____

4. man _____

5. foot _____

6. child _____

Next Step   Write the plural of each word below. Then write a
sentence using the plural form of the word.

1. *singular:* bush   *plural:* _____

sentence: _____

_____

2. *singular:* nurse   *plural:* _____

sentence: _____

_____

3. *singular:* woman   *plural:* _____

sentence: _____

_____

4. *singular:* goose   *plural:* _____

sentence: _____

_____

5. *singular:* giant   *plural:* _____

sentence: _____

_____

Name _____

Writing Numbers

Write Source Link

- Numbers from one to nine are usually written as words.

    Runner Marion Jones won five Olympic medals in one year.

- Numbers larger than nine are usually written as numerals.

    The United States has won 46 world titles in figure skating.

TIP: A number at the beginning of a sentence is written as a word.

 1 Follow the directions for each sentence. Write your numbers correctly and be sure to use your handbook.

1. Write a sentence telling how old you are.

_____

2. Write a sentence using a very large number.

_____

3. Write a sentence about the number of doors in your classroom.

_____

4. Write a sentence naming an amount of money.

_____

5. Write a sentence telling how many students are wearing tennis shoes in your class.

_____

Name _____

Using Abbreviations

An **abbreviation** is the shortened form of a word or phrase. Many abbreviations begin with a capital letter and end with a period.

Write Source Link

480, 482

Mister = Mr.
Doctor = Dr.
Street = St.

1   **Circle the abbreviations in this address:**

Mr. Michael Carlson, Jr.

222 W. Bridge Ave.

Greenville, NY   01209

TIP: Postal abbreviations for states have two capital letters and no period.

Massachusetts ·········→ MA

Next Step   **Write your name and address here. Use at least two abbreviations.**

_____
(Name)

_____
(Street)

_____
(City, State, ZIP)

Name _____

State Abbreviations

Each state has a postal abbreviation that has two letters.

Write Source Link

482

Alabama = AL   Minnesota = MN

Wyoming = WY   Maine = ME

1 After each set of clues, write the full name of the state. Then write the two-letter abbreviation for the state. The first one has been done for you.

1. Statue of Liberty, Empire State Building, Niagara Falls   New York   NY

2. Sunshine State, Kennedy Space Center, Everglades _____ _____

3. Lone Star State, Alamo, Dallas _____ _____

4. San Francisco, redwoods, the gold rush _____ _____

5. St. Louis, Gateway Arch, Lake of the Ozarks _____ _____

6. Phoenix, Grand Canyon, desert _____ _____

7. Chicago, Abe Lincoln, Lake Michigan _____ _____

8. Atlanta, Peach State, Civil War _____ _____

9. Islands, volcanoes, 50th state _____ _____

10. Santa Fe, astronomy, Carlsbad Caverns _____ _____

2   **Make your best guess to answer each question below. Then open your handbook to pages 482 and 483 to check and correct your work.**

Which is the . . .   State Name   Abbreviation

1. largest state?   _____   _____

2. smallest state?   _____   _____

3. state with the highest point? _____   _____

4. state with the rainiest spot? _____   _____

5. state with the driest desert? _____   _____

Next Step   **Draw a map of your state. Show the state capital, the city or town you live in, and other interesting places. Label your map with the state's name and its postal abbreviation.**

Name _____

Write Source Link
470-483

Mechanics Review

This activity is a review of capitalization, plurals, numbers, and abbreviations.

1 Fill in the blanks in the sentences below. Make sure to use capital letters and numbers correctly.

1. _____ is a state I want to visit.

2. _____ is my favorite holiday, and

_____ is my favorite month.

3. The abbreviation of my favorite month is _____ .

4. There are _____ students in my class.

5. Many third graders are _____ years old.

6. One of my textbooks is called _____ ,

and I am on chapter _____ .

7. My handbook is called _____ ,

and one chapter is called " _____ ."

8. There are _____ pages in *Write Source*.

2 Rewrite the addresses below, using as many abbreviations as you can.

Doctor Lee Strong _____

142 South Jefferson Drive _____

River City, Wisconsin 54999 _____

Mister Charles Johnson, Junior _____

3730 Azalea Street West _____

Wellington, South Carolina 29777 _____

3 Write the plural form of each word below. Write it under the rule that explains how to make it plural. The first one has been done for you.

bee	cow	lady	crunch	splash
cook	kitty	mess	kite	fly

1. Plurals of most nouns are made by adding an *s*.

bees _____   _____

_____   _____

2. If a noun ends in *sh, ch, x, s,* or *z,* make the plural by adding *es.*

_____   _____   _____

3. If a noun ends in *y* with a consonant just before the *y,* change the *y* to *i* and add *es.*

_____   _____   _____

Name _____

Write Source Link

487

Spelling and Alphabetizing

1 Rewrite the list of birds, putting them in alphabetical (ABC) order.

robin	cardinal	eagle
seagull	penguin	hawk
falcon	ostrich	loon
albatross	wren	tern
bluebird	vulture	duck

1. _____

2. _____

3. _____

4. _____

5. _____

6. _____

7. _____

8. _____

9. _____

10. _____

11. _____

12. _____

13. _____

14. _____

15. _____

2 Write the words in alphabetical (ABC) order. When words begin with the same letter, be sure to look at the second and third letters of the words.

1. drive, dressed, dumb

_____

_____

_____

2. toward, truth, tonight

_____

_____

_____

3. might, middle, minute

_____

_____

_____

4. bright, bunch, built

_____

_____

_____

5. planet, picture, phone

_____

_____

_____

6. pencil, past, person

_____

_____

_____

Next Step On your own paper, write an alphabet poem about something you see or hear around you. See page 291 in *Write Source* for alphabet poems about a parrot and bear cubs.

Name _____

Spelling and Silent Letters

1 Choose a word from the list to fill in each blank below. After you write the word, circle the silent consonant or consonants. The first one has been done for you.

autumn	island	night
calf	knee	rhyme
castle	lamb	write
gnat	listen	

1. The sun shines by day and the moon by _____ ni(gh)t _____ .

2. A baby sheep is called a _____ .

3. When your teacher is talking, it's important to _____ .

4. Another name for fall is _____ .

5. A king and a queen are sure to live in a _____ .

6. A baby cow is called a _____ .

7. Poems and songs often have words that _____ .

8. A _____ is a tiny bug.

9. It's fun to _____ letters to friends far away.

10. Your leg bends at the _____ .

11. An _____ is a piece of land surrounded by water.

2 Sort the words below into three groups: one-syllable words, two-syllable words, and three-syllable words.

answer	Friday	knife	right
bought	ghost	middle	science
different	happiness	neighbor	special
dressed	hurry	often	weather
dumb	interest	president	whole
finally	kitchen	probably	would

One-Syllable Words

1. _____   5. _____

2. _____   6. _____

3. _____   7. _____

4. _____   8. _____

Two-Syllable Words

1. _____   6. _____

2. _____   7. _____

3. _____   8. _____

4. _____   9. _____

5. _____   10. _____

Three-Syllable Words

1. _____   4. _____

2. _____   5. _____

3. _____   6. _____

Name _____

Spelling Sorts

1 Sort the words below into two groups. First list all the words that have double consonants. Then list all the words that have silent consonants.

answer	finally	mirror	tonight
bought	ghost	often	worry
different	guess	really	wrong
dressed	hurry	right	
dumb	knife	science	

Words with Double Consonants

1. _____   5. _____

2. _____   6. _____

3. _____   7. _____

4. _____   8. _____

Words with Silent Consonants

1. _____   6. _____

2. _____   7. _____

3. _____   8. _____

4. _____   9. _____

5. _____   10. _____

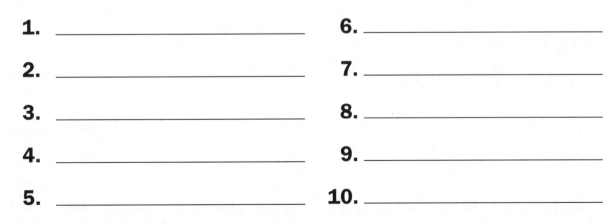

2 **Using the spelling words on pages 487, 488, and 490 in *Write Source,* write the answers to these riddles.**

1. The first meal of the day _____

2. The United States _____

3. The opposite of awake _____

4. Sounds the same as the word "right" _____

5. The opposite of picked up _____

6. 10 X 0 equals . . . _____

7. Land surrounded by water _____

8. The first month of the year _____

9. The last month of the year _____

10. The day after today _____

11. One of three blind mice _____

12. The opposite of wrong _____

13. A synonym for "fast" _____

14. A writer of books _____

15. The plural of "child" _____

Next Step **Using the words from the list, write a short story that could make someone laugh.**

Name _____

Using the Right Word 1

Write Source Link

494

Homophones are words that sound the same but have different spellings and meanings. Let's look at two homophones.

I ate a sandwich.

Eight players were sick yesterday.

The grizzly bear is a big animal.

There is a bare spot on the lawn.

1   **Write the correct word in each blank.**

1. Jermaine says he likes to watch the old polar _____ at the zoo.

2. Yesterday, the polar _____ _____ three huge fish.

3. He counted _____ blue jays trying to get the scraps.

4. The polar _____ found a _____ spot in the grass to lie

down after dinner.

Next Step   **Write one sentence using each of these words: *bear,* *bare, ate,* and *eight.***

_____

_____

_____

_____

Name _____

Write Source **Link**
496

Using the Right Word 2

Homophones are words that sound alike but have different spellings and different meanings.

Don't break the glass.
The bike's front brake is loose.

Joe likes to swim in the creek.
There is a creak in the wooden floor.

1 **Write the correct word from the list in each blank.**

break   brake   creek   creak

1. Jamie caught a big fish in the _____.

2. At first, he thought the fish would _____ his fishing line.

3. He set the _____ on the fishing reel.

4. Suddenly, he heard his old fishing rod _____.

5. When Jamie lifted the fish out of the water, he was sure it was the

biggest fish in the _____.

Next Step **In a few sentences, write a little story that uses these four words: *break, brake, creek,* and *creak.***

Name _____

Using the Right Word 3

Homophones are words that sound alike but have different spellings and meanings.

The hole in the gound is deep.
She bought the whole set of books.

I hear a rooster crowing.
Bill is here today.

Write Source **Link**

498

1 | **Write the correct word in each blank.**

hole   whole   hear   here

1. Liu's mom said, "I _____ it's going to rain all day.

2. Liu brought out a board game that the _____ family could

play.

3. He pulled the box off the shelf in his room and was surprised to see

that it had a big _____.

4. All of a sudden the box lid moved, and he could _____

something inside the box.

5. He lifted the lid and saw that his hamster had chewed up a

_____ set of score sheets.

6. "How did the hamster get _____ from his cage?" he wondered.

Name

_____

Write Source **Link**
500

Using the Right Word 4

Homophones are words that sound alike but have different spellings and meanings. Let's look at two sets of common homophones: *its, it's* and *meat, meet.*

It's vacation time.

Our school needs its summer "checkup."
(*It's* stands for it is; *its* shows ownership.)

Some people don't eat red meat

At recess, I will meet you by the swings.

1   **Write the correct word—*it's* or *its*—in each blank.**

1. Our gym needs _____ clock fixed.

2. _____ always slow.

3. We never know when _____ time to go back to our classroom.

4. Our gym needs _____ water fountain checked, too.

2   **Write the correct word—*meat* or *meet*—in each blank.**

1. Some restaurants use the best _____ to make hamburger.

2. Jolene plans to _____ Cari at the library.

3. Will you _____ me in the lunchroom?

4. What kind of _____ do you put in chili?

Name _____

Using the Right Word 5

Homophones are words that sound alike but have different spellings and meanings.

A pear is a tasty fruit.

Franklin put on his brown pair of socks.

Jill's mother will pare the carrots for stew.

The snow-coverd mountain made a beautiful scene.

Have you seen my school books?

1   **Use *pear, pair,* or *pare* to fill in the blanks.**

1. Will someone _____ the apples for me?

2. The camp said I should bring a _____ of hiking boots.

3. The _____ is still too green to eat.

4. This _____ of pictures will fit on this wall.

2   **Write *scene* or *seen* to fill in the blanks.**

1. I have _____ that movie at least three times.

2. The heavy rain hid the hilly _____ below the cabin.

3. Jan has _____ this display already.

Next Step   **Write a sentence for each of the following words:**
pair and *seen.*

Name
_____

Using the Right Word 6

Write Source Link

504

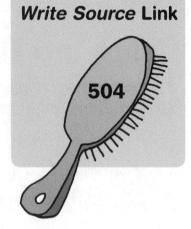

Homophones are words that sound the same but have different spellings and meanings. Let's look at five common homophones: *there, their, they're* and *tail, tale.*

I put my hairbrush there.

The girls need their hairbrushes.

They're brushing their hair.

When a cat is scared, the hair on its tail puffs up.

George told us a tale about birds using hair for nests.

1 Write the correct word—*there, their, they're* and *tail* or *tale*—in each blank.

1. _____ are about 100,000 hairs on your head.

2. Rapunzel is a _____ about a woman with very long hair.

3. _____ always falling out—from 25-125 hairs a day.

4. _____ are many kinds of hair.

5. Many people wish _____ hair was curly.

6. Some men lose _____ hair and become bald.

7. Some hairdos are named after the _____ of a pony or a pig.

8. Tell me a _____ about a woman with bright green hair.

Next Step Write a sentence for each of the following words: *there, they're,* and *tale.*

Name
_____

Using the Right Word 7

Write Source Link

Homophones are words that sound alike but have different spellings and different meanings. Let's look at some common homophones: *two, to, too* and *your, you're*.

For two years, Harry went to the chili contest.

Matilda went, too.

The chili was too hot for Harry.

Is this your bowl of chili?

You're supposed to eat the chili now.

 1 Write the correct word—*too, two, to, your,* or *you're*—in each blank.

1. This year, Matilda wanted _____ go to the chili contest.

2. She said to Harry, "I hope _____ going to go with me."

3. He said, "I have already been there _____ times."

4. He thought three times would be _____ much.

5. He wanted _____ see the frog-jumping contest instead.

6. He said to Matilda, "_____ welcome to come with me."

7. Matilda said, "It would be fun if _____ of us go."

8. She told Harry, "_____ frog contest was fun, but I'm hungry."

9. So then they went _____ the chili contest.

Name

Using the Right Word Review

Write Source Link 494-506

 If the underlined homophone in each sentence is used incorrectly, cross it out and write the correct word above it. The first one has been done for you.

1. I have ~~ate~~ *eight* shoelaces.

2. Jon saw a <u>bare</u> at the wildlife park.

3. Be careful not to <u>break</u> that glass bowl.

4. Because of the heavy rain, the <u>creak</u> is flooding.

5. I think <u>its</u> going to rain all night.

6. I gave my mom a new <u>pair</u> of slippers for her birthday.

7. Have you <u>seen</u> the new movie about Sammy the Seal?

8. Did you <u>here</u> about our field trip to the orange-juice factory?

9. Bob's cat ate a <u>hole</u> bowl of tuna salad that was on the counter.

10. Billy has <u>too</u> buckets to make sand castles at the beach.

11. Do you have <u>you're</u> ticket for the movie?

12. That squirrel has a very stubby <u>tail</u>.

13. <u>There</u> are several empty boxes in the hallway.

2

Sentence
Activities

This section includes activities related to basic sentence writing, kinds of sentences, sentence problems, and sentence combining. The Next Step activities often require original writing.

Name _____

Simple Subjects and Predicates

Write Source Link 398, 510, 512

The **subject** of a sentence names someone or something. The **simple subject** is the main word in the subject.

The **predicate** (verb) tells what the subject is or does. The **simple predicate** is the main word in the predicate.

simple subject   simple predicate

The new <u>bike</u> <u>gleams</u> in the sun.

---

1 **Fill in each blank with a word that makes sense. Each word you add will be the simple subject of the sentence.**

1. _____ takes piano lessons.

2. _____ walks to school.

3. _____ wag their tails when they are happy.

4. _____ stampeded across the prairie.

---

2 **Fill in each blank with a word that makes sense. Each word you add will be the simple predicate of the sentence.**

1. Ryan _____ spaghetti.

2. The teacher _____ us a story.

3. The sun _____ bright today.

4. Susie _____ soccer.

3 In each sentence below, underline the simple subject once and underline the simple predicate twice. The first sentence has been done for you.

1. <u>Diana</u> <u>plays</u> first base.

2. The thunder scared Timmy.

3. Schuyler lives next door.

4. Pizza is my favorite food.

5. Maria won.

6. Peter did the dishes.

7. Summer is the best time of year.

8. Our bus comes at 8:00 a.m.

Next Step Think of three people you know. Write one sentence about each person. Each sentence should tell something the person is or does. Underline the simple subject of each sentence once and the simple predicate twice.

1. _____

_____

2. _____

_____

3. _____

_____

Name _____

Subject of a Sentence

Write Source Link

396, 510

● Every sentence has a subject. The **subject** of a sentence names something or someone.

My old friend jumped over the candlestick.

(*My old friend* is the complete subject.)

● The **simple subject** is the main word in the subject.

My old friend jumped over the candlestick.

(*Friend* is the simple subject.)

● A **compound subject** is made up of two or more simple subjects.

Jack and Jill jumped over the candlestick.

(*Jack* and *Jill* make up the compound subject.)

1   Draw a line under each complete subject. Circle each simple subject. The first one has been done for you.

1. A few little (seeds) fell to the ground.

2. An enormous beanstalk grew up and up.

3. Brave Jack climbed the beanstalk.

4. A huge castle rose up out of the clouds.

5. The ugly giant roared, "Fee, fie, fo, fum!"

6. The giant's wife saved Jack.

7. An old clock protected Jack from the giant.

8. Frightened little Jack stayed very still.

2 Draw a line under the complete subject in each sentence below. Write an *S* in the blank if the main part of the subject is simple or a *C* if the main part is compound. The first one has been done for you.

__C__ **1.** The giant and his wife ate dinner.

_____ **2.** The ugly giant called for his magic goose.

_____ **3.** The magic goose laid golden eggs.

_____ **4.** The giant and the goose slept.

_____ **5.** Jack snatched the goose.

_____ **6.** The bold boy climbed down the beanstalk.

_____ **7.** The surprised giant chased him.

_____ **8.** Jack's mother chopped down the beanstalk.

_____ **9.** Jack and his mother lived happily ever after.

Next Step Write three sentences about a favorite fairy tale. Underline the complete subject in each sentence you write.

1. _____

_____

2. _____

_____

3. _____

_____

Name _____

Predicate of a Sentence

Write Source Link

397, 512

- The **predicate** (verb) of a sentence tells what the subject is or does.

  Maya <u>writes stories on her computer.</u>

  (*Writes stories on her computer* is the complete predicate.)

- The **simple predicate** is the main word in the predicate.

  Maya <u>writes</u> stories on her computer.

  (*Writes* is the simple predicate.)

- A **compound predicate** is made up of two or more simple predicates.

  Maya <u>writes</u> stories and <u>plays</u> music on her computer.

  (*Writes* and *plays* make up the compound predicate.)

1 Draw two lines under each complete predicate. Circle each simple predicate, or verb. The first one has been done for you.

1. Maya (thinks) of good stories.

2. Maya writes about a magic keyboard.

3. The keyboard creates 100-page stories overnight.

4. Everybody loves the stories.

5. She wins dozens of prizes.

6. She becomes a great author.

7. Maya wants a magic keyboard like this.

2 Draw two lines under the complete predicate in each sentence below. Write an *S* in the blank if the main part of the predicate is simple. Write a *C* if the main part of the predicate is compound.

_____C_____ **1.** Maya <u><u>sings and composes music</u></u>.

_____ **2.** Maya composes music on her computer.

_____ **3.** She plays the melody and sings the words.

_____ **4.** Maya's friends join her.

_____ **5.** They sing old songs and make up new ones.

_____ **6.** Maya's dog sings, too.

_____ **7.** The dog barks and howls.

_____ **8.** Maya's mother listens to the singing.

_____ **9.** She smiles and shakes her head.

_____ **10.** She joins in the fun.

_____ **11.** Everyone has a good time.

Next Step Complete each thought below. Draw two lines under the complete predicates in your sentences.

The best computer game _____

_____.

My friends and I _____

_____.

Name _____

Subject and Predicate Review

Write Source Link 396–399, 510, 512

1 In these sentences, underline each simple subject once and underline the simple predicate twice. The first one has been done for you.

1. Betty Bodette drives a red convertible.

2. My father drives a truck.

3. The truck belongs to a landscaping company.

4. I ride with my father sometimes.

5. My big sister comes, too.

6. We help my father.

7. He treats us to lunch at noon.

2 Put a check in the subject box if the sentence has a compound subject. Put a check in the predicate box if the sentence has a compound predicate.

COMPOUND	
Subject	Predicate
✔	

1. Betty and her sister drive to the mall.

2. Betty buys a sundae and goes to the movies.

3. Betty and her sister like funny movies.

4. Her brother skateboards and plays video games.

5. He and his friends like to ride in the convertible.

3 Change each sentence so it has a compound subject. You will also have to change the predicate so that it agrees, or makes sense, with the new subject. The first one has been done for you.

1. Jeff walks to school.

Jeff and Jared walk to school.

2. Caroline rides on the bus.

_____

3. Mrs. Hodorowski likes to take the train.

_____

4. I walk with my friend Luz.

_____

4 Change each sentence so it has a compound predicate.

1. The Lone Ranger rides a horse.

The Lone Ranger rides a horse and shoots silver bullets.

2. Mary Poppins flies with her umbrella.

_____

_____

3. Superman soars over the city.

_____

Name _____

Simple and Compound Sentences 1

- A **simple sentence** has one main thought.
  You have two eyes.

- A **compound sentence** is two simple sentences
  joined by a comma and a connecting word
  (such as *and, but,* or *so*).
  You have two eyes, <u>and</u> they both see the same thing.

1 Carefully read the following sentences. Write an *S* in the
blank for each simple sentence and a *C* for each compound
sentence. The first two have been done for you.

___*S*___ **1.** Miss Filbert loves science.

___*C*___ **2.** She talked about eyesight, and then she did an experiment.

_____ **3.** Miss Filbert threw a ball to Peter, and he threw it back to her.

_____ **4.** She caught the ball.

_____ **5.** Then she put on an eye patch.

_____ **6.** Peter threw the ball again.

_____ **7.** Miss Filbert reached out to catch the ball, but she missed it.

_____ **8.** Miss Filbert made an important point.

_____ **9.** Two eyes help us see in 3-D, and they help us catch a ball.

2 Combine each set of simple sentences to make a compound sentence. The first one has been done for you.

1. Some eyes are blue. Some eyes are brown.

 Some eyes are blue, and some eyes are brown.

2. A horse has two eyes. They are on the sides of its head.

_____

_____

3. A human has simple eyes. A dragonfly has compound eyes.

_____

_____

4. Fish see underwater. Many of them see in color.

_____

_____

Next Step Write one simple sentence and one compound sentence about your eyes.

Simple Sentence:

_____

_____

Compound Sentence:

_____

_____

Name _____

Simple and Compound Sentences 2

Write Source Link

408

- A **simple sentence** has one main thought. (Although it may have two subjects or two verbs.)

  Jerry <u>wrote</u> a poem.

  (This simple sentence has one subject and one verb.)

  <u>Jerry</u> and <u>Talia</u> <u>wrote</u> a poem.

  (This simple sentence has two subjects and one verb.)

  <u>Jerry</u> <u>wrote</u> a poem and <u>drew</u> a picture.

  (This simple sentence has one subject and two verbs.)

- A **compound sentence** is two simple sentences joined by a comma and a connecting word.

  <u>Jerry</u> and <u>Talia</u> <u>wrote</u> a poem, **and** <u>I</u> <u>read</u> it.

  (This compound sentence expresses two thoughts.)

1 Carefully read each sentence. Write an *S* in the blank for each simple sentence and a *C* for each compound sentence. (*Hint:* A compound sentence must have a comma and a connecting word such as *and, or, but,* or *so.*)

_____ **1.** Marisa and Tom read the same book.

_____ **2.** Charlie drew a picture and gave it to me.

_____ **3.** I cleaned the hamster cage, and Anthony watered the plants.

_____ **4.** The teacher and parents had a meeting.

_____ **5.** Brittany forgot her sweater, so I loaned her mine.

_____ **6.** It started to rain, and we closed the windows.

2   **Write the following types of sentences about things that have happened in your classroom.**

1. Write a simple sentence with one subject and one predicate (verb).

_____

_____

2. Write a simple sentence with two subjects and one verb. (Your sentence will be about two people who did one thing.)

_____

_____

3. Write a compound sentence. (Your sentence will be two simple sentences joined with a comma and a connecting word.)

_____

_____

4. Write one more compound sentence about your class.

_____

_____

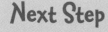 **Next Step**   **Trade papers with a partner. Read and check each other's sentences. Make sure you followed directions correctly.**

Name _____

Write Source Link

409

Declarative and Imperative Sentences

- A **declarative sentence** makes a statement.

  Leroy is a beagle.

- An **imperative statement** gives a command or makes a request.

  Leroy, sit.

  Declarative sentences and imperative sentences both end with periods.

1 Read each sentence carefully. Write *D* before each declarative sentence and *I* before each imperative sentence.

_____ **1.** Leroy is 13 years old.

_____ **2.** Thirteen is old for a dog.

_____ **3.** Leroy, go get the newspaper.

_____ **4.** Roll over, boy.

_____ **5.** Leroy snores.

_____ **6.** Leroy takes liver-flavored vitamins.

_____ **7.** Take your vitamin, Leroy.

2 Draw a picture of Leroy the dog. Then write some sentences about him. Write two declarative sentences that tell about Leroy. Write two imperative sentences that tell Leroy to do things.

Declarative sentences:

1. _____

_____

2. _____

_____

Imperative sentences:

1. _____

_____

2. _____

_____

Name _____

Kinds of Sentences

Write Source Link

409

- A **declarative sentence** makes a statement.
  Michaelangelo was a sculptor.

- An **imperative sentence** gives a command or makes a request.
  Ask your teacher what a sculptor does.

- An **interrogative sentence** asks a question.
  Should we carve a bar of soap?

- An **exclamatory sentence** shows strong emotion or surprise.
  That's a great idea!

1 Carefully read the sentences below. Then tell what kind of sentence each one is. Write *D* for a declarative sentence, *IN* for an interrogative sentence, *IM* for an imperative sentence, and *E* for an exclamatory sentence. The first one has been done for you.

___D___ **1.** Sculptors make figures in stone or clay.

_____ **2.** Do you know any other sculptors?

_____ **3.** Donatello was a sculptor.

_____ **4.** I don't believe it!

_____ **5.** Look it up if you don't believe me.

_____ **6.** Michaelangelo studied Donatello's sculptures.

_____ **7.** What was so great about Donatello?

2 Turn each statement into a question. Add or drop words, or change the order of the words to make your new sentences. The first one has been done for you.

1. Michaelangelo lived in Italy.

Did Michaelangelo live in Italy?

2. Michaelangelo lived about 500 years ago.

_____

3. Michaelangelo was a painter and a sculptor.

_____

4. Many artists copy Michaelangelo's works.

_____

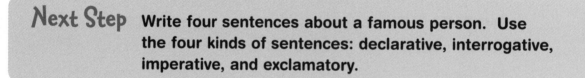

Next Step Write four sentences about a famous person. Use the four kinds of sentences: declarative, interrogative, imperative, and exclamatory.

Declarative: _____

_____

Interrogative: _____

_____

Imperative: _____

_____

Exclamatory: _____

_____

Name _____

Write Source Link

401

Sentence Fragments 1

A complete sentence has a subject and a predicate. If either one or both of these are missing, you have a **sentence fragment**.

● In this sentence fragment, the subject is missing.

Fragment: Jumped off the diving board.

Corrected Sentence: Jeb jumped off the diving board.
(A subject has been added.)

● In this sentence fragment, the subject and verb are missing.

Fragment: In the pool.

Corrected Sentence: Jenna and Jane swam in the pool.
(A subject and verb have been added.)

 1 Write a *C* in front of each complete sentence below, and write an *F* in front of each sentence fragment. The first one has been done for you.

_____F_____ **1.** An excellent swimmer.

_____ **2.** Herman is an excellent swimmer.

_____ **3.** Breaststroke, Australian crawl, and backstroke.

_____ **4.** He is teaching me how to swim.

_____ **5.** I am leaving.

_____ **6.** Because of the weather.

2 Correct each sentence fragment below.

1. In the ocean.

Missy McGee swims in the ocean.

2. Bought scuba equipment.

3. Below the surface.

4. Colorful fish everywhere.

5. Because of the sharks.

6. Reached the boat.

Next Step Read the fragments and your sentences to a partner. Listen to the difference between a fragment and a complete sentence.

Name _____

Sentence Fragments 2

Remember, a complete sentence has a subject and a predicate. If either one or both are missing, you have a **sentence fragment**.

401

1 **Read the paragraphs below. (If possible, read aloud with a partner.) Then underline each sentence fragment.**

Two Orphan Cubs by Erika Kors. A true story about two bear cubs. One day their mother left them forever. Gary Alt found the cubs in the den. Very hungry and lonely. Put the little bears into a sack. Took the bears to Molly's den. Molly was a bear and had two of her own cubs.

A great story. I liked it. Because there was a happy ending.

2 **Rewrite the paragraphs, using complete sentences.**

_____

_____

_____

_____

_____

_____

_____

_____

Name _____

Sentence Fragments 3

When you are using the word *because* in a sentence, make sure you don't end up with a fragment. To make a sentence, the word *because* must be combined with two complete thoughts.

Fragment: Because it had a happy ending.

Corrected Sentence: I liked it because it had a happy ending.

---

1 Make each sentence fragment below into a complete sentence.

1. _____ because I missed lunch.

2. _____ because she is sick.

3. _____ because it is my birthday.

4. _____ because I lost my socks.

5. My friend was late because _____ .

6. I can't go because _____ .

7. He's happy because _____ .

8. I'm sorry because _____ .

Next Step Write a complete sentence on the lines below using the word *because.*

_____

_____

Name _____

Run-On Sentences 1

Write Source Link

402

A **run-on sentence** happens when two or more sentences run together.

Run-On Sentence:
Mr. Wiggle's lawn mower needs repair he can't fix it.

Corrected Sentences:
Mr. Wiggle's lawn mower needs repair. He can't fix it.
(two sentences)

Mr. Wiggle's lawn mower needs repair, but he can't fix it.
(compound sentence)

 1 Change each of these run-on sentences into two sentences.

1. He pulled the cord the engine didn't start.

He pulled the cord.   The engine didn't start.

2. His grass was growing fast dandelions were popping up.

_____

_____

3. Mr. Wiggle borrowed our mower he has not returned it yet.

_____

_____

4. I hope he gives it back soon our grass is getting very long.

_____

_____

2 Correct each run-on sentence below by rewriting the run-on as a compound sentence. (See *Write Source* 166.) The first one has been done for you.

1. Mr. Witt toasted some bread it burned.

   Mr. Witt toasted some bread, but it burned.

2. The smoke set off a fire alarm the fire department came.

_____

3. Mr. Witt was surprised to see the firefighters he told them what happened.

_____

_____

4. Mr. Witt threw out the toaster Mrs. Witt pulled it from the trash.

_____

_____

5. Mr. Witt bought a new toaster his wife fixed the old one.

_____

_____

6. Now the Witts have two toasters we're thinking of borrowing one.

_____

_____

Next Step Pair up with a classmate and check each other's compound sentences. Make sure your partner has placed a comma before the connecting word in each of his or her sentences.

Name _____

Run-On Sentences 2

A run-on sentence happens when two or more sentences run together.

Run-On Sentence:
We read about Vikings they were smart.

Corrected Sentences:
We read about Vikings. They were smart.

Write Source **Link**

402

1 Change each run-on sentence into two sentences.

1. The Vikings came to North America before Columbus they were the first Europeans to come here.

_____

_____

2. Vikings were also called Norsemen northern Europe was their home.

_____

_____

3. The Vikings were good sailors they were also warriors.

_____

_____

4. Once Vikings sailed to England their ships sailed up a river to London.

_____

_____

2 Correct each run-on sentence by rewriting it as a compound sentence. See handbook page 408.

1. Eric the Red led Vikings to Greenland his son Leif later led Vikings to Canada.

_____

_____

2. No one knows why they sailed to Canada there were no towns there to raid.

_____

_____

3. Some experts think they were fishing a storm blew their ships off course.

_____

_____

Next Step Write two run-on sentences about a topic you are studying. Your sentences can be serious or silly. Trade papers with a partner and correct each other's run-ons.

1. _____

_____

2. _____

_____

Name
_____

Combining Sentences with a Key Word

Write Source Link

406

One way to combine sentences is to move a **key word** from one sentence to the other.

Short Sentences: Lizzie plays basketball.
She is on the fifth-grade team.

Combined Sentence: Lizzie plays on the (fifth-grade) basketball team.
(The key word is circled.)

---

1 Circle the key word or words that were used to make a combined sentence. The first one has been done for you.

1.   **Short sentences:**   Her team has new uniforms.
They are blue and white.

Combined sentence: Her team has new (blue and white) uniforms.

2.   **Short sentences:**   Ms. Charleyhorse is the coach.
She coaches basketball.

Combined sentence: Ms. Charleyhorse is the basketball coach.

3.   **Short sentences:**   The team goes to away games in a van.
The van is brand-new.

Combined sentence: The team goes to away games in a brand-new van.

4.   **Short sentences:**   Laura cheers for Lizzie's team.
She cheers loudly.

Combined sentence: Laura cheers loudly for Lizzie's team.

2 Combine each set of sentences below by moving a key word or words from one sentence to the other.

1. Jesse loves to roller-skate. He roller-skates every day.

_____

_____

2. Jesse sometimes uses his brother's roller skates. The roller skates are green.

_____

_____

3. Jesse likes to roller-skate with his friends. He has five friends.

_____

_____

4. His friends are going to roller-skate with him. They will roller-skate tomorrow.

_____

_____

5. Everyone will practice for a race. The race will be long.

_____

_____

Next Step Write two short sentences about one of your favorite activities. Combine your ideas into one longer sentence. (Use your own paper for your work.)

Name

Combining Sentences with a Series of Words or Phrases 1

Write Source Link

406

Short Sentences: I like camping.
I like hiking.
I like swimming.

Combined Sentence: I like camping, hiking, and swimming.

1 Fill in the blanks to complete each group of short sentences. Then combine each group to make one longer sentence.

1. I like to play _____ .

I like to play _____ .

I like to play _____ .

Combined sentence: _____

_____

2. I like to read _____ .

I like to read _____ .

I like to read _____ .

Combined sentence: _____

_____

2 In the space below, draw a picture of a make-believe animal. Then use words in a series to write sentences about your animal.

1. Write a sentence telling three things your animal likes to eat.

_____

_____

2. Write a sentence telling three places your animal likes to hide.

_____

_____

3. Write a sentence telling three things your animal can do.

_____

_____

Name _____

Combining Sentences with a Series of Words or Phrases 2

Write Source Link

392, 406

You can combine short sentences that tell different things about the same subject.

Short Sentences: George Washington Carver was curious. He was smart. He was hardworking.

Combined Sentence: George Washington Carver was curious, smart, and hardworking.

(The three words in a series tell different things about the subject.)

1 Combine these sentences using a series of words or phrases.

1. As a boy, George Washington Carver worked as a cook. He worked as a launderer. He worked as a janitor.

_____

_____

2. In the laboratory, Carver found new ways to use peanuts. He found new ways to use pecans. He found new ways to use sweet potatoes.

_____

_____

3. Carver made ink from sweet potatoes. He made flour from sweet potatoes. He made rubber from sweet potatoes.

_____

_____

2 Combine these sentences by using a key word from one sentence or by using words or phrases in a series.

1. Thomas Edison invented a lightbulb. He invented a phonograph. He invented a movie camera.

_____

_____

2. Edison asked questions that began with "why." He asked questions that began with "how."

_____

_____

3. Edison's inventions were easy to use. They were easy to keep in order. They were easy to fix.

_____

_____

4. He worked long hours and took only naps. The naps were short.

_____

Next Step Thomas Edison made improvements in many modern inventions, including batteries, typewriters, microphones, telephones, and radios. Write a sentence naming three of the things he helped to improve.

_____

_____

_____

Name _____

Combining Sentences with Compound Subjects and Verbs 1

Write Source Link

399, 407

Short Sentences: LaJoy went to the circus.
Kelly went to the circus.

Combined Sentence: LaJoy and Kelly went to the circus.

(*LaJoy* and *Kelly* make up a compound subject.)

* * * * * * * *

Short Sentences: LaJoy went to the circus.
She watched the clowns.

Combined Sentence: LaJoy went to the circus and watched the clowns.

(*Went* and *watched* make up a compound verb.)

1 Draw lines under the compound subject or the compound verb in each combined sentence.

1. **Short sentences:** Tim likes the trapeze artists.
Henry likes the trapeze artists.

Combined sentence: Tim and Henry like the trapeze artists.

2. **Short sentences:** High-wire performers ride bikes.
They walk on their hands.

Combined sentence: High-wire performers ride bikes and walk on their hands.

3. **Short sentences:** Aerialists hang by their teeth.
They twirl around.

Combined sentence: Aerialists hang by their teeth and twirl around.

2 Combine each pair of sentences using a compound subject or a compound verb.

1. Kelly munched popcorn. She gobbled peanuts.

_____

_____

2. Hector wanted cotton candy. His brother wanted cotton candy, too.

_____

_____

3. LaJoy bought balloons. Tim also bought balloons.

_____

_____

4. Kelly bought a clown wig. She stuck it on her head.

_____

_____

Next Step Write two sentences about a circus. In one sentence, use a compound subject. In the other sentence, use a compound verb.

Compound Subject: _____

_____

Compound Verb: _____

_____

Name

Combining Sentences with Compound Subjects and Verbs 2

Write Source Link 399, 407

Here's more practice using compound subjects and verbs to combine sentences.

 Combine each group of sentences using a compound subject or verb. The first one has been done for you.

1. Once a hen lived on a farm. A cat also lived on the farm. A pig also lived on the farm.

Once a hen, a cat, and a pig lived on a farm.

2. The hen gathered some wheat. The hen ground some wheat.

_____

3. The cat refused to help her. The pig refused to help her, too.

_____

4. The hen baked two loaves of bread. The hen ate two loaves of bread.

_____

5. The cat begged for some bread. The pig begged for some, too.

_____

2 Write two sentences about the animals in the story on page 109. Use compound subjects in both of your sentences. Then write two more sentences about the animals, using compound verbs.

Sentences with compound subjects:

1. _____

   _____

2. _____

   _____

Sentences with compound verbs:

1. _____

   _____

2. _____

   _____

Next Step Draw a picture about one of your sentences.

Name _____

Sentence Combining Review 1

Write Source Link 406–408

 Combine each group of sentences with a key word or a series of words or phrases

1. Many students ride to school. Many students ride buses.

_____

2. Students laugh on the bus. Students sing on the bus. Students talk on the bus.

_____

3. Students carry books. Students carry lunches. Students carry pencils.

_____

4. The students get off the bus. The students go into the school. The students sit down in class.

_____

_____

5. The bus seats are covered with plastic. The plastic is green.

_____

6. Many school buses are painted. Many school buses are orange.

_____

_____

2 Combine the groups of sentences using compound subjects and verbs.

1. Some trees live for thousands of years. Some trees grow for thousands of years.

_____

_____

2. Sequoias are very large trees. Redwoods are every large trees.

_____

3. These trees shade the soil. These trees protect the soil.

_____

4. The man photographed redwood trees. The man climbed redwood trees.

_____

5. Adults are amazed at the size of a sequoia. Children are amazed at the size of a sequoia.

_____

6. You would look tiny next to a sequoia. I would look tiny next to a sequoia.

_____

_____

Name _____

Write Source Link
406–408

Sentence Combining Review 2

 1 Combine each group of sentences into one longer sentence. You can do this by moving the underlined words into the first sentence. (Sometimes you need to add the word *and*.)

1. You may have noticed that bears have tails. Their tails are <u>short</u>.

_____

2. According to legend, bears once had tails that were long. They had tails that were <u>bushy</u>. They had tails that were <u>beautiful</u>.

_____

_____

3. Then one day a bear saw a fox. The fox was <u>clever</u>.

_____

4. The fox was eating crayfish. He was <u>licking his lips</u>.

_____

5. The bear asked the fox how to catch crayfish. The bear was <u>hungry</u>.

_____

6. The fox told the bear to chop a hole in the ice. He told the bear to <u>put his tail in the hole</u>.

_____

_____

2 Continue combining the two sentences into one longer sentence. You can do this by moving the underlined words into the first sentence. (Sometimes you need to add the word *and*.)

1. The fox told the bear to sit and wait. He told the bear to wait <u>until a crayfish grabbed his tail.</u>

_____

_____

2. The bear went down to the frozen river. <u>The fox</u> went, too.

_____

3. The bear followed the fox's instructions. The bear was <u>trusting.</u>

_____

4. The ice froze around the bear's tail. It froze <u>quickly.</u>

_____

5. The bear had to leave his tail in the ice. The ice was <u>thick.</u>

_____

6. That is why bears have tails that are short. Their tails are <u>stubby.</u> Their tails are <u>not beautiful.</u>

_____

_____

Next Step On your own paper, write three short sentences telling what you think of the fox in this story. Then see if you can combine two or more of your sentences to make a longer sentence.

Language Activities

3

The activities in this section are related to the eight parts of speech. All of the activities have a page link to *Write Source*.

Name _____

Nouns

A **noun** names a person, a place, a thing, or an idea. The following lists are nouns that belong to each of the four groups.

373, 516

Person	Place	Thing	Idea
bride	street	bicycle	joy
boy	pool	flowerpot	truth
friend	school	horse	hope
coach	park	whale	sadness

1 Complete each sentence below by adding nouns from the lists above. (Your sentences can be as silly as you want to make them.) The first one has been done for you.

1. The _____ bride _____ hopped over the _____ flowerpot _____.

2. My _____ tells the _____.

3. The _____ is in the _____.

4. A _____ has lots of _____.

5. The _____ sang to the _____.

6. Look at the _____ riding a _____.

7. John told his _____ to go to the _____.

8. Myra saw a _____ on the _____.

9. The _____ is full of _____.

2 Draw a line under the two nouns in each of these sentences. The first sentence has been done for you.

1. The <u>clown</u> sings in the <u>bathtub</u>.

2. The gorilla rides a skateboard.

3. The chef cooked a buzzard.

4. That kid lives in Overshoe.

5. The cowboy roped a skunk.

6. Sarah sang with joy.

7. This path leads to the cave.

8. Mary dreamed of flying cows.

9. The runner has lots of hope.

Next Step Draw a picture for one of the sentences you worked with in this activity.

Name _____

Common and Proper Nouns

Write Source Link

373, 516

- A **common noun** names any person, place, thing, or idea.

  man   country   book

- A **proper noun** names a specific person, place, thing, or idea.

  Mr. Taylor   Mexico   Write Source

 1 Match each group of proper nouns to a common noun. The first one has been done for you.

Common Nouns

_h_ **1.** states

____ **2.** songs

____ **3.** countries

____ **4.** mountains

____ **5.** lakes

____ **6.** boys

____ **7.** planets

____ **8.** languages

____ **9.** rivers

____ **10.** books

Proper Nouns

a. Canada, Mexico, United States

b. Venus, Mars, Earth

c. Lake Michigan, Great Salt Lake, Lake Okeechobee

d. Steve, John, Jim

e. Rocky Mountains, Blue Ridge Mountains, Ozark Mountains

f. "The Star-Spangled Banner," "America the Beautiful," "This Land Is Your Land"

g. Missouri River, Snake River, Yukon River

h. Hawaii, Alaska, California

i. English, Spanish, Mandarin Chinese

j. *Write on Track, Strega Nona, Where the Wild Things Are*

2 After each common noun, write a proper noun that goes with it. Your proper nouns can name real people, places, and things, or they can be made-up names.

Common Nouns   **Proper Nouns**

1. doctor _____

2. cat _____

3. park _____

4. book _____

5. store _____

6. girl _____

7. team _____

8. city _____

9. river _____

10. movie _____

11. boy _____

12. teacher _____

Next Step On your own paper, write a paragraph using some of the nouns above. After you finish, label each common noun *C* and each proper noun *P*.

Name

Singular and Plural Nouns

Write Source Link

374, 518

● A **singular noun** names one person, place, thing, or idea.

farmer   park   car   freedom

Write two more singular nouns here.

_____   _____

● A **plural noun** names more than one person, place, thing, or idea.

farmers   parks   cars   freedoms

Write two more plural nouns here.

_____   _____

1 Draw one line under each noun in the sentences below. Label each singular noun *S* and each plural noun *P*. The first one has been done for you.

1. My children work in the theater.
    _P_   _S_

2. Elizabeth acts in plays.

3. Her brother paints the sets.

4. The theater is on Hill Street.

5. Two new shows just opened.

6. Sean had free tickets.

7. The audience laughed at the jokes.

2 Write five singular nouns in the first column. Then write the plural of each noun in the second column.

singular   plural

1. _____   _____

2. _____   _____

3. _____   _____

4. _____   _____

5. _____   _____

Write two interesting sentences using singular nouns from your list.

1. _____

_____

2. _____

_____

Write two interesting sentences using plural nouns from your list.

1. _____

_____

2. _____

_____

Name _____

Write Source Link

375, 518

Possessive Nouns 1

A possessive noun is a noun that shows ownership. To make a singular noun possessive, add an apostrophe and an *s*. (Singular means one.)

The tree frog's skin is rough and green.
My teacher's aquarium holds two frogs.

1 Circle each possessive noun. Underline what belongs to it. The first one has been done for you.

1. The frog lives on the (pond's) shore.

2. Frog eggs float on the water's edge.

3. Tadpoles hatch from a frog's eggs.

4. A tadpole's color changes as it grows.

5. A frog can balance on a tree's leaf.

6. Pet frogs need the owner's care.

7. Mr. Juarez's tank is a mini jungle.

2 Change the following words into singular possessive nouns.

1. rock   a _____ color

2. mountain   that _____ peak

Name _____

Write Source Link
375, 518

Possessive Nouns 2

The plural possessive is used to show ownership. Add an apostrophe after the *s* of most plural nouns to make them possessive.

Chorus frogs' songs sound like a choir.

1 Circle the correct word in parentheses to finish each sentence below.

1. You will hear the *(peeper's, peepers')* voices first in the spring.

2. In some places, *(coyote's, coyotes')* howls join in.

3. *(Owl's, Owls')* hoots add to the nightly concerts.

4. Hundreds of *(cricket's, crickets')* songs ring out, too.

2 Fill in the plural possessive nouns in the chart below.

	Noun	Singular Possessive Noun	Plural Possessive Noun
1.	boat	boat's	
2.	tree	tree's	
3.	forest	forest's	
4.	lake	lake's	

Name _____

Personal Pronouns 1

A **pronoun** is a word that takes the place of a noun.

Sam wrote a letter and mailed it.

(The pronoun *it* replaces the noun *letter*.)

Sam opened the mailbox, and he found a letter from Andy.

(The pronoun *he* replaces the noun *Sam*.)

Write Source Link

377, 520

U.S. MAIL

Common Personal Pronouns

Singular Pronouns

I, me, my, mine
you, your, yours
he, him, his, hers
she, her, it, its

Plural Pronouns

we, our, us, ours
you, your, yours
they, their, them, theirs

 1 In each sentence below, change the crossed-out names to a personal pronoun. The first one has been done for you.

1. Tracy and Gaby started a newspaper, and ~~Tracy and Gaby~~ they write all the stories.

2. Gaby uses ~~Gaby's~~ mom's computer.

3. Tracy and Gaby interviewed the teacher, and ~~the teacher~~ told ~~Tracey and Gaby~~ about her new piano.

4. The teacher told Tracy and Gaby about ~~the teacher's~~ music lessons.

5. The girls like the idea that ~~the girls'~~ teacher is learning new things.

6. Gaby said, "~~Tracy and Gaby~~ like our teacher a lot."

2 Circle the correct personal pronoun in parentheses for each sentence. The first one has been done for you.

1. Jerome told the girls about *(her, his)* teacher.

2. Jerome said *(his, he)* reading teacher is a soccer coach.

3. The teacher coaches when *(he, him)* is done with school.

4. *(His, ours)* team is happy to have a fair coach.

5. Jerome and Andre learn from *(them, their)* coach.

6. He teaches *(their, them)* to be good sports.

Next Step Write four sentences about a class or a teacher you enjoy. Underline the personal pronouns in your sentences.

_____

_____

_____

_____

_____

_____

_____

Name _____

Personal Pronouns 2

A **pronoun** is a word that replaces a noun.

Write Source Link
520

1 In each of the sentences, write the name of the person that the underlined pronoun stands for. Write <u>Lori</u> or <u>Pam</u>.

One day Lori was playing kickball in the backyard.

1. After a few minutes, <u>she</u> heard Pam calling <u>her</u>.

_____   _____

2. Pam was calling from <u>her</u> yard, but Lori couldn't see <u>her</u>.

_____   _____

3. Lori called, "Do <u>you</u> want to play kickball with <u>me</u>?"

_____   _____

4. "<u>I</u> sure do," answered Pam. And <u>she</u> ran right over.

_____

2 Fill in personal pronouns for the next part of the story.

Lori and Pam had lots of fun. When _____ finished

playing kickball, the girls went into the house. Lori's mom gave

_____ a treat. Pam said, "Thank _____.

_____ sure had fun at _____ house today."

3 Circle all of the pronouns you find in this paragraph. (There are 19 pronouns all together.)

Living with a Little Brother

Living with (my) little brother can be hard. First, he tries to copy me. If I have a second glass of milk, he does, too. Second, he always wants to play with my friends. If we play basketball, he wants to join in. But he is too small. Third, he wants to stay up as long as I do. He always says to my mom, "But Tim gets to stay up later." My mom says that he looks up to me, and I should be proud to be his big brother.

Next Step Write a short paragraph about someone in your family. Circle all of the pronouns you use.

_____

_____

_____

_____

_____

_____

_____

Name
_____

Pronouns: I and Me, They and Them

Write Source Link
377

A **pronoun** is a word that replaces a noun. *I* and *me* are pronouns. *They* and *them* are also pronouns.

I is used as the subject of a sentence.
 I lost the key.

Me is used after an action verb or after a preposition.
 Angelo called me. Mom baked cookies for me.

They is used as the subject of a sentence.
 They are friends.

Them is used after an action verb or after a preposition.
 The lightning scares them. Sophie had a surprise for them.

1 Write the correct word, *I* or *me*, in each blank.

1. _____ need a haircut.

2. Daniel called _____.

3. Janelle asked _____ for a marker.

4. _____ finished my homework.

5. Carla did my chores for _____.

2 Write the correct word, *they* or *them,* in each blank.

1. I invited _____ to my party.

2. _____ like to read stories.

3. I visit _____ every Saturday.

4. We made a present for _____.

5. _____ are my cousins.

3 Choose the correct word from each pair and write it in the blank.

_____ made two bracelets and gave _____ to
(I, Me)   (they, them)

Maggie. _____ are made from glass beads. My sister showed
(They, Them)

_____ how to make _____. Maggie's parents told
(I, me)   (they, them)

_____ the bracelets were very pretty. _____ said
(I, me)   (They, Them)

_____ should keep making _____. _____
(I, me)   (they, them)   (They, Them)

said _____ could sell _____ at the craft show.
(I, me)   (they, them)

4 Write three sentences about a game you play with a friend. Use as many pronouns as you can.

1. _____

_____

2. _____

_____

3. _____

_____

Name

_____

Possessive Pronouns

A **possessive pronoun** shows ownership. It can be used before a noun.

Our street has a new name.

My street is now called King Drive.

Write Source **Link**

378, 520

1   **Choose a word from the list below to complete each sentence. Use each word only once.**

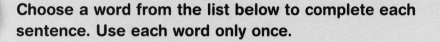

my   your   his   her   its   our   their

1. The house at 410 Oak Street is _____ house.

2. That's _____ house on the corner.

3. Matt rides _____ skateboard around the block.

4. Our neighbors painted _____ house yellow.

5. Mrs. Acker has a gravel driveway at _____ house.

6. The house is big, and three cars can fit in _____ garage.

7. What does _____ house look like?

2   **Write about your neighborhood. Use at least three words from the list above in your sentences.**

_____

_____

3 Finish each sentence with the best choice from the list below.

theirs   yours   his   hers   ours   mine

1. This journal is _____.

2. Tom put a picture of a galaxy on _____ journal's cover.

3. Sherrie has stickers on _____.

4. Tim and I share this basket of pencils. It is _____.

5. Another group has a basket of markers. It is _____.

6. Take this pencil if it is _____ .

Next Step Write two sentences about items that belong to other people. Use two possessive pronouns from the list above.

1. _____

_____

2. _____

_____

Name _____

Action and Linking Verbs

Write Source Link

381, 382, 522

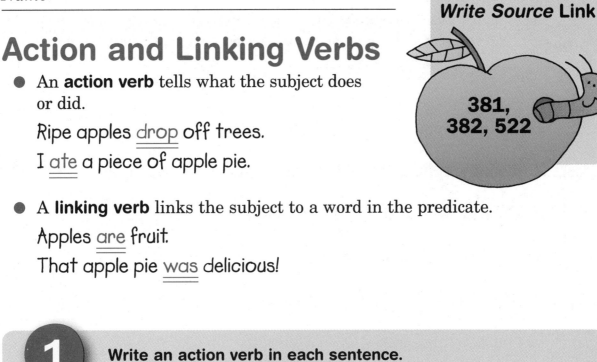

● An **action verb** tells what the subject does or did.

Ripe apples <u>drop</u> off trees.

I <u>ate</u> a piece of apple pie.

● A **linking verb** links the subject to a word in the predicate.

Apples <u>are</u> fruit.

That apple pie <u>was</u> delicious!

---

1 **Write an action verb in each sentence.**

1. Apple trees _____ in late spring.

2. I _____ apples in the fall.

3. Once I _____ a worm in an apple.

4. My mom _____ apple butter.

---

2 **Write a linking verb in each sentence.**

1. Applesauce _____ soft and delicious.

2. Granny Smith apples _____ green.

3. I _____ an apple fan!

4. Last year, the orchard _____ full of apples.

3 Draw two lines under the verb in each sentence. Write an *A* in the blank if the verb shows action or an *L* if the verb links two words. The first one has been done for you.

___A___ **1.** Johnny Appleseed <u><u>learned</u></u> about apples.

_____ **2.** Johnny Appleseed's real name was John Chapman.

_____ **3.** Johnny walked through the Midwest.

_____ **4.** He wore a sack as a shirt.

_____ **5.** He planted many, many apple trees.

_____ **6.** Johnny Appleseed was well-known.

_____ **7.** Many people wrote books about him.

_____ **8.** Some books about Johnny Appleseed are tall tales.

Next Step Write three sentences about apples. Use at least one of the verbs below in each sentence.

eat   peel   chop   cut   taste   is   be   are   was   slice

1. _____

_____

2. _____

_____

3. _____

_____

Name _____

Helping Verbs

A **helping verb** comes before the main verb and helps to state an action or show time.

Helping Verbs: can, could, did, do, had, has, have, may, should, will, would

Write Source Link
383, 522

 1 Draw two lines under the helping verb and action verb in each sentence. The first one has been done for you.

1. Parrots <u>can sleep</u> standing up.

2. Humpback whales do make a lot of noise.

3. Australians have named baby kangaroos "joeys."

4. A baby elephant will grow quickly.

5. Swans do eat plants, insects, and small fish.

 2 Write two sentences. Each sentence should contain one of the action verbs listed below, plus a helping verb. Draw two lines under each helping verb and action verb.

run   push   eat   called

Example: An elephant <u>can eat</u> a lot.

1. _____

_____

2. _____

_____

Name
_____

Verb Review 1

Write Source Link
381–383, 522

- There are two main types of verbs, **action verbs** and **linking verbs**.

  I <u>fed</u> my dog. (*Fed* is an action verb.)

  He <u>is</u> hungry. (*Is* is a linking verb.)

- Sometimes a **helping verb** is used with an action verb or a linking verb.

  My dog <u>will eat</u> anything.

1 Draw two lines under the main verb in each sentence. Write an *A* in the blank if the verb shows action or an *L* if the verb links two words. The last two sentences contain helping verbs. For those sentences, underline the helping verbs along with the main verbs.

___A___ **1.** My dog <u>runs</u> fast.

_____ **2.** My dog acts like a person.

_____ **3.** His name is Bob.

_____ **4.** We are so happy with Bob.

_____ **5.** He plays in the kitchen.

_____ **6.** My baby sister Nina loves Bob.

_____ **7.** She sits in the kitchen with him.

_____ **8.** Once she tasted Bob's dog food.

_____ **9.** Nina should eat her own food!

_____ **10.** Bob will be our friend forever.

Name _____

Verb Tenses 1

● A verb in the **present tense** tells you that the action takes place now, or that it happens all the time.

I <u>hear</u> a cricket singing.

A cricket <u>hops</u> across the lawn.

● A verb in the **past tense** tells you that the action happened in the past.

Yesterday a cricket <u>hopped</u> onto my leg.

1 Carefully read each sentence. Write "present" in the blank if the underlined verb is in the present tense, or "past" if it is in the past tense.

____present_____ **1.** Crickets <u>sing</u> by rubbing their wings together.

_____ **2.** My grandfather <u>keeps</u> a singing cricket in a cage.

_____ **3.** It <u>tells</u> the temperature.

_____ **4.** On hot days it <u>chirps</u> fast.

_____ **5.** I <u>heard</u> the cricket chirp a few minutes ago.

_____ **6.** It <u>chirped</u> 50 times in 15 seconds.

_____ **7.** I <u>tried</u> to chirp myself.

_____ **8.** I <u>sounded</u> really stupid.

_____ **9.** Chirping <u>gives</u> me a sore throat.

2 Each present-tense verb in the following sentences is underlined. On each blank, write the past tense of the verb. Then read the sentence with the new verb in it.

Present Tense	**Past Tense**
1. My friends <u>find</u> crickets in the spring.	_found_
2. Sometimes they <u>keep</u> them as pets.	
3. On cold days, the circkets <u>chirp</u> slowly.	
4. My friends and I <u>like</u> bugs.	
5. We <u>see</u> the bug display at the museum.	
6. The largest bug <u>hisses</u> loudly.	
7. It <u>grows</u> to about four inches long.	
8. I <u>enjoy</u> studying insects	

Next Step Write two sentences about insects. Use a present-tense verb in one sentence and a past-tense verb in the other.

Present tense: _____

_____

Past tense: _____

_____

Name _____

Verb Tenses 2

385,
524

● Remember that a verb in the **present tense** tells you that the action takes place now, or that it happens all the time.

It snows.

I make a snowman.

● A verb in the **future tense** tells you that the action will take place at a later time.

The sun will come out.

It will melt the snow.

---

1 After each sentence, check whether the underlined verb is in the present tense or in the future tense. The first one has been done for you.

	PRESENT	FUTURE
1. I <u>see</u> snow falling.	✔	
2. Snow <u>falls</u> softly and silently.		
3. It <u>covers</u> roads and roofs.		
4. I <u>hope</u> that it snows all night.		
5. Then they <u>will close</u> the schools.		
6. I <u>will have</u> to shovel snow.		
7. I <u>will clear</u> the walk.		
8. Then I <u>will build</u> a snow fort.		
9. That <u>sounds</u> like fun!		

2 Draw two lines under the verb in each sentence. Write "present" in the blank if the verb is in the present tense, "future" if it is in the future tense. The first one has been done for you.

future   **1.** What <u><u>will melt</u></u> snow?

_____   **2.** Salt melts snow.

_____   **3.** Dan's experiment will prove it.

_____   **4.** Dan fills two cans with snow or ice.

_____   **5.** He dumps salt on the snow in one can.

_____   **6.** He sets a timer for one hour.

_____   **7.** Then he will look at the cans.

Next Step Change each of the following sentences to the future tense. Then write one more sentence about snow. Use the future tense in your new idea.

1. Snow falls.

_____

2. It clings to branches and twigs.

_____

3. Soon the world looks like a giant wedding cake.

_____

4. _____

_____

Name _____

Verb Tenses 3

The **tense** of a verb tells you if the action happened in the present, past, or future.

Present Tense:

Peter <u>picks</u> a peck of pickled peppers.

Past Tense:

Peter <u>picked</u> a peck of pickled peppers yesterday.

Future Tense:

Peter <u>will pick</u> a peck of pickled peppers tomorrow.

Write Source Link

384, 385
524

1 Draw two lines under the verb in each of the following tongue twisters. Then, in the blank space, write "past," "present," or "future" for the tense of the verb. The first sentence has been done for you.

_____past_____ **1.** A big black bug <u>bit</u> a big black bear.

_____ **2.** Three gray geese grazed in the green grass.

_____ **3.** Teddy took two turtles to Todd's house.

_____ **4.** Barbara always burns the brown bread.

_____ **5.** A fly flew through the flue.

_____ **6.** The dog will choose to chew the shoes.

_____ **7.** She will sip a cup of hot cinnamon cider.

_____ **8.** I love little lightning bugs.

_____ **9.** Carol collects colorful cups.

Present	Past	Future
run	ran	will run
sells	sold	will sell
close	closed	will close
bubbles	bubbled	will bubble
take	took	will take
watch	watched	will watch

Create your own tongue twisters by completing the sentences below. Select verbs from the list above. The first one has been done for you.

1. The ragged rascal _____ran_____ around the rocks.
(past)

2. She _____ seashells by the seashore.
(past)

3. Rosie and Rory _____ around the roller rink.
(present)

4. Clyde's Clothes Closet _____ for cleaning.
(future)

5. Double bubble gum _____ double.
(future)

6. Tim _____ a turn on Tammy's tandem.
(past)

7. Wally _____ the walrus in the water.
(past)

Next Step Share your tongue twisters with a classmate. Write more examples to share. (Use your own paper.)

Name _____

Write Source Link

Regular Verbs

- Add *-ed* to regular verbs to form the past tense.

  Willy and Milly <u>sailed</u> the boat last summer.

- Also add *-ed* to regular verbs when you use a helping verb such as *has, have,* or *had.*

  Willy <u>had sailed</u> for years.

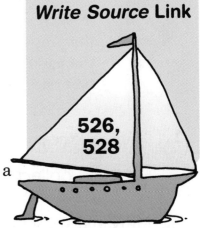

526, 528

* * * * * * * * *

- If a regular verb ends in *e*, just add *d* to form the past tense.

  raise ·······➤ raise<u>d</u>

- If a one-syllable verb ends in a single consonant, double the consonant and add *-ed*.

  shop ·······➤ shop<u>ped</u>

---

1 **Write these regular verbs in the past tense.**

1. hop _____hopped_____

2. hope _____

3. name _____

4. tap _____

5. skip _____

6. raise _____

7. talk _____

8. hum _____

9. push _____

10. save _____

11. flip _____

12. splash _____

13. stop _____

14. giggle _____

15. lick _____

16. drip _____

2 In each set of sentences below, study the underlined verb in the first sentence. Then write the -*ed* (past tense) form of the underlined verb to complete the second sentence. The first one has been done for you.

1. They <u>call</u> the boat the *Lilly*.

They _____*called*_____ it the *Lilly* two years ago.

2. Milly and Willy <u>row</u> out to the *Lilly*.

Yesterday, they _____ out to the *Lilly*.

3. Milly <u>raises</u> the *Lilly's* sail.

Last year, she _____ it every morning.

4. Milly and Willy <u>love</u> to sail the *Lilly*.

Milly and Willy always have _____ to sail the *Lilly*.

5. Milly <u>drops</u> the anchor.

Willy gave the signal, and Milly _____ the anchor.

6. Willy <u>cleans</u> the *Lilly* once a week.

He had _____ it two days before the storm.

Next Step Draw a picture including Milly, Willy, and the *Lilly*.

Name _____

Singular and Plural Verbs

The subject of a sentence can be singular or plural. Notice how the verb *plays* changes when the subject changes from singular to plural.

Write Source Link

386, 526

Caleb <u>plays</u> basketball at the park.
(singular verb)

His friends <u>play</u> with him.
(plural verb)

1   **Write the correct form of the verb in each sentence.**

1. practices   practice

Jake, Caleb, and Rhonda _____ shooting baskets every day.

Sometimes Jake even _____ at night.

2. dribbles   dribble

Caleb _____ the ball across the court.

Then Jake and Rhonda _____ it.

3. tosses   toss

Rhonda _____ the ball, and she misses.

Caleb and Jake _____ and miss.

4. jumps   jump

The boys _____ for the rebound.

Rhonda _____ , too.

2 Write your own sentences using the singular and plural verbs listed.

1. passes   pass

_____

_____

2. scores   score

_____

_____

3. cheers   cheer

_____

_____

4. joins   join

_____

_____

5. chooses   choose

_____

_____

Next Step Draw two lines under all of the singular verbs. What do you notice about all of them?

Name _____

Irregular Verbs

526, 528

1 Study the irregular verbs in the handbook. As a class, complete the sentences below with the correct forms of the irregular verb.

1. begin

    present: I _____ school at 8:30.

    past: Last year, school _____ at 8:00.

    past with *had:* When I got there, school had _____.

2. am

    present: I _____ in the third grade.

    past: Last year, I _____ in second grade.

    past with *have:* I have _____ looking forward to third grade.

3. catch

    present: I _____ a lot of balls at softball practice.

    past: In my last game, I _____ a fly ball.

    past with *had:* I had _____ two fly balls in other games.

4. hide

    present: I _____ from my brother sometimes.

    past: Last night, I _____ in my closet.

    past with *have:* I have _____ there before.

2 Now complete the following sets of sentences on your own. The directions are the same as in part 1.

1. fly

present: I _____ to Minneapolis every summer.

past: Last year, I _____ by myself.

past with *have:* I have _____ for years with my dad.

2. come

present: Most days, I _____ to school with my sister.

past: Yesterday, I _____ by myself.

past with *have:* I have _____ by myself two other times.

3. throw

present: I _____ practice pitches every Friday.

past: Last Friday, I _____ 30 pitches.

past with *had:* I had _____ 25 pitches before I hurt my arm.

Next Step Write two sentences of your own using different forms of the verb *speak.*

1. _____

_____

2. _____

Name _____

Verb Review 2

An **action verb** tells what someone or something does.

Jenny <u>hits</u> lots of home runs.

The wind <u>blows</u> down our fort.

Write Source **Link**
381, 522, 526

 1 List three action verbs below. Trade papers with a partner. Then write two sentences for each of your partner's action verbs—one singular and one plural.

1. Action verb: _____
Sentence with singular verb:

_____

Sentence with plural verb:

_____

2. Action verb: _____
Sentence with singular verb:

_____

Sentence with plural verb:

_____

3. Action verb: _____
Sentence with singular verb:

_____

Sentence with plural verb:

_____

2 In the paragraph below, change each underlined verb to past tense. The first one has been done for you.

rang
Dennis <u>rings</u> the doorbell and then <u>runs</u> away and <u>hides</u>. I <u>see</u> him

and <u>tell</u> my mom. She <u>says</u> Dennis <u>does</u> it because he <u>likes</u> me. Maybe

she <u>is</u> right. Dennis also <u>rides</u> his bike past our house and <u>brings</u> our

newspaper to the door.

Next Step Write some more sentences about Dennis, using the verbs given. First write a sentence in the present tense. Then write a sentence in the past tense.

1. Verb: write

Sentence in present tense: _____

_____

Sentence in past tense: _____

_____

2. Verb: go

Sentence in present tense: _____

_____

Sentence in past tense: _____

_____

Name _____

Write Source Link
387, 530

Adjectives 1

● An **adjective** usually comes before the noun it describes.

Carrie planted tiny seeds.

What noun does the adjective
tiny **describe in this sentence?** ___seeds___

● Sometimes an **adjective** comes after a linking verb.

The seeds were tiny.

What noun does the adjective
tiny **describe in this sentence?** ___seeds___

1   Underline the adjective in each sentence. Then draw an arrow to the noun it describes. (Don't include the words *a, an,* or *the*.) The first one has been done for you.

1. She used a <u>sharp</u> spade to dig.

2. Carrie planted red zinnias.

3. She watered the little seeds.

4. Green leaves soon popped up.

5. Bright sun shone on the plants.

6. Gentle rain watered them.

7. Fat buds formed.

8. Soon Carrie could pick a pretty bouquet of zinnias.

2 Draw a line under each adjective in the following sentences. Then draw an arrow to the noun it describes. All of these adjectives come after a linking verb. The first one has been done for you.

1. Roses are <u>red</u>.

2. Violets are blue.

3. Sugar is sweet.

4. Words are true.

5. Daisies are white.

6. Marigolds are yellow.

7. Honey is sweet.

8. Sarah sure is mellow.

Next Step Write a sentence for each adjective-noun pair.

Adjectives	Nouns
fluffy ·············>	kitten
tough ·············>	guy
beautiful ·············>	song
silver ·············>	earrings

1. _____

_____

2. _____

_____

3. _____

_____

4. _____

_____

Name _____

Write Source Link

382, 387

Adjectives 2

An **adjective** is a word that describes a noun or a pronoun.

● An **adjective** usually comes before the noun it describes.

Auntie Grimelda has blue hair.

(*Blue* describes *hair.*)

● Sometimes an **adjective** comes after a linking verb.

Auntie Grimelda's hair is blue.

1 On your own paper, draw a picture of a person. Imagine that this person is going to be the main character in a fantasy story. Put lots of details in your drawing. Use lots of colors. (And give your person a name.) After you finish, list adjectives below to describe the person you drew.

hair	face	eyes
_____	_____	_____
_____	_____	_____

nose	mouth	ears
_____	_____	_____
_____	_____	_____

body	clothes	voice
_____	_____	_____
_____	_____	_____

2 Trade pictures and your list of adjectives with a classmate. Look closely at your partner's drawing. Add some adjectives to your partner's list.

Next Step Trade papers again so that you have your own drawing and the adjectives that describe it. Write a paragraph that describes the person you drew. Use as many of your adjectives as you can.

Name _____

Proper Adjectives

An adjective formed from a proper noun is called a **proper adjective**.

America has a flag.

(*America* is a proper noun.)

The American flag is red, white, and blue.

(*American* is an adjective that describes the flag.)

1 Circle the proper adjectives in the sentences below.

1. The (English) language contains words from many places.

2. *Medicine* is a French word.

3. A German teacher created the word *kindergarten*.

4. The word *pretzel* comes from the German language.

5. *Moose, chipmunk,* and *opossum* are Native American words.

6. The Scandinavian people first used the word *egg*.

7. *Chimpanzee* and *banana* are words from African countries.

Next Step Think of a food that comes from another country. Use a proper adjective in a sentence describing that food.

_____

_____

Name _____

Compound Adjectives

Write Source Link
530

A **compound adjective** is made up of more than one word. Some compound adjectives are spelled as one word. Some words are spelled with a hyphen.

We got drinks at the **drive-up** window.

Match the following words to create compound adjectives. Write them on the lines.

_____ **1.** house   color

_____ **2.** old   fashioned

_____ **3.** hard   mother's

_____ **4.** grand   ware

_____ **5.** water   hold

Fill in each blank with the best choice from the words you created above.

1. Roseanna visits her _____ house in summer.

2. Grandma Maria lives next to the _____ store.

3. Roseanna helps Grandma with _____ chores.

4. Roseanna loves Grandma's big, _____ couch.

5. Over the couch is a giant _____ painting of a forest.

Name _____

Forms of Adjectives

Adjectives have three different forms.

Positive: This pebble is small.

Comparative: This pebble is smaller than that rock.

Superlative: This pebble is the smallest stone in my collection.

Write Source Link

388, 532

1   Write sentences for the forms of the adjectives listed below.

loud, louder, loudest

1. _____

2. _____

   _____

3. _____

   _____

happy, happier, happiest

1. _____

2. _____

   _____

3. _____

   _____

2 Write a paragraph about a beautiful or interesting place you have visited. Use plenty of adjectives in your writing.

_____

_____

_____

_____

_____

_____

_____

_____

_____

_____

_____

Next Step Circle the adjectives in your paragraph. Did you write any adjectives in the comparative (ending in -*er*) or the superlative form (ending in -*est*)?

Name _____

Adverbs 1

An **adverb** is a word that describes a verb, or tells how an action is done. Adverbs usually tell *when, where,* or *how.*

Write Source Link

- Some adverbs that tell *when:*

  always   never   soon   weekly

- Some adverbs that tell *where:*

  outside   there   up

- Some adverbs that tell *how:*

  slowly   loudly   jokingly

1 Circle the adverb in each sentence. Then write whether it tells *when, where,* or *how.* The first one has been done for you.

1. Jeremy (always) eats his cabbage. _____ when _____

2. Karen goes to bed early. _____

3. Rags comes quickly when he is called. _____

4. Shari never teases her little brother. _____

5. Todd goes to the dentist cheerfully. _____

6. Michelle cleans her room daily. _____

7. I took the trash outside. _____

8. Sean makes his bed carefully. _____

9. Emily comes here for lunch. _____

2 Cross out the adverb in each sentence. Replace it with a different adverb that changes the meaning of the sentence. The first one has been done for you.

1. "I'll ride a bike," Mom said ~~seriously~~. *jokingly*

2. Sparky snores softly.

3. Cal seldom sees his cousins.

4. Tamika did her chores happily.

5. Maria is never late for school.

6. "Those boys are playing so quietly," said Granddad.

7. Fuzzy stays nearby when he knows it's bath time.

Next Step Write three sentences about yourself.

1. Use the adverb *someday* (when).

_____

_____

2. Use the adverb *outside* (where).

_____

_____

3. Use the adverb *slowly* (how).

_____

_____

Name _____

Write Source **Link**

389, 534

Adverbs 2

An **adverb** is a word that describes a verb, or tells how an action is done. Adverbs usually answer *when* (adverb of time), *where* (adverb of place), or *how* (adverb of manner).

1 Adverbs of time tell *when* or *how often* an action is done. Fill in the blank in each sentence with one adverb from the list below.

yesterday	soon	now	first
tomorrow	later	weekly	last

1. Our class went to the toy museum _____.

2. I hope we can go back again _____.

3. In fact, I wish we could go _____.

2 Adverbs of place tell *where* something happens. Fill in the blank in each sentence with one adverb from the list below.

inside	here	up
outside	there	down

1. I told my mom I wanted to go _____ to play.

2. She looked _____ at me.

3. "Why don't you just play _____?" she asked.

3 Adverbs of manner tell *how* something is done. Fill in the blank in each sentence with one adverb from the list below.

quietly	carefully	slowly	happily
loudly	carelessly	quickly	sadly

1. I like to play my cassette player _____.

2. When I clean up my room, I do it very _____.

3. When it's time to eat, my cat comes running _____.

Next Step Write four adverbs. Then write a paragraph that has all four adverbs in it.

1. _____   **3.** _____

2. _____   **4..** _____

_____

_____

_____

_____

_____

_____

Name _____

Prepositions

A phrase that begins with a preposition and ends with a noun is called a **prepositional phrase**.

to the lighthouse
in the boat
under the bridge
across the water
after breakfast

Write Source Link

391, 536

---

1 Draw a line under the prepositional phrase in each sentence below. Then circle each preposition. The first one has been done for you.

1. Ray was (in) deep water.

2. Ray was swimming against the tide.

3. He went backward with every stroke.

4. Waves washed over his head.

5. He was not near the beach.

6. Just then, he felt the nudge of a boat.

7. A lifeguard threw him a life preserver on a rope.

8. Ray reached for the rope.

9. The lifeguard rowed Ray toward the beach.

10. Ray said, "Thank you. I was really in danger."

2 Draw a line under the prepositional phrases in the sentences below. Then circle each preposition. (Some of these sentences have more than one prepositional phrase.) The first one has been done for you.

1. Pay attention (to) these rules (about) water safety.

2. Swim at beaches protected by lifeguards.

3. Never jump into strange waters.

4. Always look for underwater obstacles.

5. Do not swim in unmarked areas or in bad weather.

6. Always swim close to the shore and with a friend.

7. Go slowly into cold water.

8. Swim with other people.

9. Stay inside the buoys.

Next Step Create a sign for one of the safety rules above.

Name _____

Write Source Link

392, 538

Conjunctions

A **conjunction** connects words or groups of words. The most common conjunctions are *and, but,* and *or.* There are three conjunctions in the following sentence:

Charley (and) Barbara wore their coats (and) hats, (but) they forgot their boots.

1 **Draw a circle around the 10 conjunctions in this story.**

The Sun (and) the Wind

Who is stronger, the sun or the wind? Well, once upon a time, each one thought it was stronger, so they had a contest.

"I am strong enough to make that man take off his hat, his scarf, and his coat," bragged the wind. The sun said nothing. It just hid behind a cloud.

The wind blew and blew, but the man did not take off his hat, his scarf, or his coat. Instead, he pulled them tighter and tighter to his body.

Then the sun came out brightly but quietly. Soon the man grew warm. He took off his hat, and he took off his scarf. Then he removed his coat.

Now do you know who is stronger? Is it the sun or the wind?

Next Step **Write a sentence that answers the last two questions in the story.**

_____

_____

Name

Interjections

Write Source Link

Hey! Let me tell you about interjections. An **interjection** is a word or phrase used to express strong emotion or surprise. It is usually followed by an exclamation point.

1 Draw a picture or design for each interjection and sentence. Write your own sentence with an interjection in the last box. Draw a picture for it, too.

Hey! I did it!

Wow, I can't believe I just saw that!

Yuck! Look at all the bugs!

Name _____

Parts of Speech Review 1

This activity is a review of the parts of speech.

Write Source Link
**373–393,
516–538**

 Write three examples of each part of speech. Do as many as you can on your own. Then ask a classmate for help or check *Write Source.*

Nouns
(Name a person, a place, a thing, or an idea)

_____

_____

_____

Pronouns
(Take the place of nouns)

_____

_____

_____

Verbs
(Show action or link ideas)

_____

_____

_____

Adjectives
(Describe a noun or pronoun)

_____

_____

_____

Adverbs
(Describe a verb; tell how an action is done)

_____

_____

_____

Conjunctions
(Connect words or groups of words)

_____

_____

_____

Prepositions
(Introduce a prepositional phrase)

_____

_____

Interjections
(Express strong emotion or surprise)

_____

_____

Next Step In the space below, draw a picture that shows this sentence:

The shiny red spaceship rocketed to the stars!

Copy the sentence under your drawing. Then label each word to show what part of speech it is.

Name _____

Parts of Speech Review 2

Write Source Link
373–393,
516–538

1 Fill in each blank below with a word that is the correct part of speech. Use each word only once.

in	silently	their	birds	quickly
pointed	they	worms	sharp	and
but	soars	floats	around	wow

1. Nouns: Robins are _____ that fly and eat _____ .

2. Pronouns: Finches eat _____ seeds until _____

spot a cat.

3. Verbs: A hawk _____ above, and a duck _____ in the bay.

4. Adjectives: Falcons have _____ claws and _____ beaks.

5. Adverbs: Owls hunt _____ and _____ to catch prey.

6. Conjunctions: Barn owls _____ screech owls sleep all day,

_____ they hunt at night.

7. Prepositions: Chickadees live _____ the northern United States,

and they often flock _____ seed feeders.

8. Interjections: _____ ! Birds are amazing.

2   **Read the following paragraph and follow the directions below.**

My grandmother <u>is</u> a bird-watcher. Grandma Fran and <u>I</u> spend time <u>quietly</u> watching and feeding many birds. Grandma <u>always</u> looks at <u>her</u> bird <u>book</u>. Grandma marks what kinds of birds she sees <u>in</u> a notebook. I read her <u>long</u> list and carefully <u>count</u> the different kinds. <u>Wow!</u> Dozens of birds eat <u>around</u> Grandma's backyard. <u>Grandpa</u> says Grandma has seen <u>every</u> bird in our state, <u>but</u> I know Grandma can find more. <u>Look!</u> Is that a blue jay <u>or</u> a bluebird? I bet Grandma knows.

Write the underlined words in the correct spaces. Find two examples for each part of speech.

Part of Speech	1	2
noun		
pronoun		
verb		
adjective		
adverb		
conjunction		
preposition		
interjection		